JUST A COMMON SOLDIER
(A SOLDIER DIED TODAY)

and Other Poems

by A. Lawrence Vaincourt

TRUE ENOUGH BOOKS
TORONTO, ONTARIO
CANADA

Canadian Cataloguing in Publication Data

Vaincourt, A. Lawrence (Amos Lawrence), 1923 –

   Just A Common Soldier (A Soldier Died Today)
   and Other Poems

ISBN 0-9735988-0-8

    I. Title

PS8593.A5266J88 2004   C811'.54   C2004-904173-8

True Enough Books
31 Wychcrest Avenue, Suite 100
Toronto, Ontario
Canada M6G 3X8
(416) 534-8899
www.vaincourt.homestead.com

First Printing: July 2004

By the same author:

"Rhymes and Reflections" 1991
"Don't Burn The Biffy" 1995

DEDICATION

*This volume is dedicated to five exceptional sons
and a wife who made it all possible.*

ABOUT THE BOOK

The poem *JUST A COMMON SOLDIER (A Soldier Died Today)* was originally written for the author's 1987 Remembrance Day newspaper column, and was later included in his 1991 collection *RHYMES & REFLECTIONS*.

It has since been reprinted thousands of times in newspapers and magazines, broadcast annually on national radio and television shows, and read at numerous private, government and military functions. A quick check on the internet reveals that it now appears on thousands of web sites around the world, with more being added every day.

Its appeal is obvious. It offers a poignant, touching view of the *Common Soldier* – the men and women who give of themselves unselfishly in difficult times; the ones who tend to be forgotten once the battle is done.

With this in mind we present this collection of poems, all of which first appeared in the author's column. Inside you'll enjoy over fifty original poems, heartwarming, hilarious and always touching, from the pen of A. Lawrence Vaincourt.

TABLE OF CONTENTS

PREFACE

That day, as I glanced up from my typewriter, I found myself looking at my all-time favorite of the many cameras with which I had earned my living over the many years I toiled as a professional photographer.

The camera's twin lenses, like two round eyes, stared back at me; a bit resentfully I thought, as though asking how I could abandon such a fascinating job at an age when so many of my fellow photographers were just hitting their stride. How, indeed?

Sixty was not old and yet here I was, unemployed, with no idea how I was to spend my remaining years. Then, out of the blue, a man I had never met offered me a job doing something I had never done: Writing a column for a weekly paper.

Time and endless articles later I still find myself churning them out, along with poetry I took to writing about the same time.

Of the many subjects I have written about – people, things or places – I do not believe that I have ever paid homage to a camera.

Yet this camera, spots on its surface worn bright by the pressure of my hands, spoke to me with the voice of an old and trusted friend.

I, CAMERA (p. 78)

And our work will be ever enduring
While other works, greater, will pass.
But then, I am only a Camera,
Just a thing made of metal and glass.

– Larry Vaincourt

7

INTRODUCTION

This is the time for a rippling rhyme
Or maybe a yarn or two,
To pick you up when you're feeling down
And cheer you when you're blue.
So sit right down and listen up
And hopefully you'll find,
A song to tickle your funny bone
Or a tale to warm your mind.
A bit of chaff to make you laugh
Or cheer you when you're low,
And by the way, this book is for you,
The ordinary Joe.

I dedicate this to the working stiff
Who must earn his bread by toil,
To the laborer up to his knees in muck
To the farmer who tills the soil,
To the mailman out on his wintry route
To the girl in the corner store,
To the cop on the beat with his big flat feet,
To the fellow who holds the door.

To the guy with the mop, in the midnight hour
Who has office floors to scrub,
To the waitress who smiles, though her feet are sore
As she hustles your morning grub,
To all of the workers, the unsung ones
Who make things run on time,
Yes you are the people that I salute
In story, verse and rhyme.

Chapter 1: Never Forgotten

Just a Common Soldier
(A Soldier Died Today)

He was getting old and paunchy
and his hair was falling fast,
And he sat around the Legion,
telling stories of the past.
Of a war that he had fought in
and the deeds that he had done,
In his exploits with his buddies;
they were heroes, every one.

And tho' sometimes, to his neighbors,
his tales became a joke,
All his Legion buddies listened,
for they knew whereof he spoke.
But we'll hear his tales no longer
for old Bill has passed away,
And the world's a little poorer,
for a soldier died today.

He will not be mourned by many,
just his children and his wife,
For he lived an ordinary
and quite uneventful life.
Held a job and raised a family,
quietly going his own way,
And the world won't note his passing,
though a soldier died today.

When politicians leave this earth,
their bodies lie in state,
While thousands note their passing
and proclaim that they were great.
Papers tell their whole life stories,
from the time that they were young,
But the passing of a soldier
goes unnoticed and unsung.

Is the greatest contribution
to the welfare of our land
A guy who breaks his promises
and cons his fellow man?
Or the ordinary fellow who,
in times of war and strife,
Goes off to serve his Country
and offers up his life?

A politician's stipend
and the style in which he lives
Are sometimes disproportionate
to the service that he gives.
While the ordinary soldier,
who offered up his all,
Is paid off with a medal
and perhaps, a pension small.

It's so easy to forget them
for it was so long ago,
That the old Bills of our Country
went to battle, but we know,

It was not the politicians,
with their compromise and ploys,
Who won for us the freedom
that our Country now enjoys.

Should you find yourself in danger,
with your enemies at hand,
Would you want a politician
with his ever-shifting stand?
Or would you prefer a soldier,
who has sworn to defend
His home, his kin and Country
and would fight until the end?

He was just a common soldier
and his ranks are growing thin,
But his presence should remind us
we may need his like again.
For when countries are in conflict,
then we find the soldier's part
Is to clean up all the troubles
that the politicians start.

If we cannot do him honor
while he's here to hear the praise,
Then at least let's give him homage
at the ending of his days.
Perhaps just a simple headline
in a paper that would say,
Our Country is in mourning,
For a soldier died today.

AGED WARRIOR

I have come the whole route and the journey's been grand,
From infant to childhood, from child to a man,
From a man to a father, the way nature planned,
And at last it is time to step down.

It has been a hard fight, but my fighting's near done,
And a lot of hard work, but it mostly was fun,
But I see my face now, in the face of my son,
And I know that it's time to step down.

I have never been wealthy, I have sometimes been poor,
I have lived through Depression and fought in a war,
But I like to think now, that the fighting is o'er,
And that I can rest for awhile.

But I would like to think that when I pass away,
I will leave the world better, in some little way,
Than it was as I found it, or indeed, is today;
Maybe then, I can go with a smile.

I remember so well the grand plans of my youth,
When I was so certain I knew the whole truth,
And how right must triumph, for wrong was uncouth;
But somehow, it wasn't that way.

For it seems the bad guys are still winning the fight,
They keep changing the rules about what's wrong and right,
You're a hero at dawn, but a villain by night,
And priorities change day by day.

From the sword to the plowshare is such a long span,
For it seems that to fight is the nature of man,
And it just hasn't worked out the way that I planned;
For the cunning still rule with their guile.

And the strong and the wealthy still prey on the poor,
But each generation must fight its own war,
So I'll hang up my sword and do battle no more;
Maybe then, I can rest for awhile.

THE REGIMENTAL SOLDIER

If you met him dressed in civvies
you would pass him with a smile,
He's a regular Joe, an ordinary man,
But because he is a soldier
he's the guy that you must hate,
And it is your job to kill him if you can.

He has never done you evil,
he's a normal guy like you,
Has a home he loves, some children and a wife,
But because he wears a uniform
that's different from your own,
It's your duty to deprive him of his life.

He's an ordinary fellow,
yes he's quite a decent guy,
And to have him as a friend might have been fun,
He could be married to your sister
had the circumstance been changed,
But now you must destroy him with a gun.

He's the regimental soldier,
just an ordinary man
Who's been told his duty is to go and fight,
And he'll kill a total stranger,
someone he has never met,
'Cause they told him you are wrong and he is right.

No, he didn't start the war you fight,
he'd rather live in peace,
He had enough to satisfy his need,
It's the evil politicians
with their senseless lust for power,
And a mad desire to satisfy their greed.

It's the ones who build the weapons,
it's the ones who lust for fame,
It's the ones who hate, without a reason why,
Who support the awful carnage
that the world still knows as War,
And who feel it's right that someone else should die.

For it's not the sons of wealthy men
who march away to war,
Who struggle on the battlefield and die,
In the same sad tale repeated
through the centuries, more and more,
It's the offspring of the ordinary guy.

And so someone is the victim,
someone strikes the mortal blow,
With each convinced that he is in the right,
And I'm sure the final battle
that this world will ever know,
Is the one where politicians have to fight.

THOUGHTS IN FLIGHT

I soar where birds have never flown,
    on massive silver wings,
And think of flights that I have known,
    on flimsy fabric things.

A piston engine's throaty roar,
    an airscrew's throbbing cry,
A little, open yellow plane
    that bore me to the sky.

With plastic coupe-top overhead
    and cables 'neath my feet,
With instruments before my face
    and parachute for seat.

For thus it was that first I learned
    the thrill it was to fly,
And be akin to all the things
    that filled the windswept sky.

The flash of gleaming, yellow wings
    cavorting through the air,
The pride of knowing that my skills
    had helped to put them there.

My job it was to service them
    and keep them in the sky,
But how I envied other men
    who had the skills to fly.

A stewardess at my elbow now,
  with nod and friendly smile,
And drink in hand, and I smile back
  and leave my thoughts awhile.

Considering this mighty ship,
  so graceful in its flight,
That spans a continent in hours
  and gets me home by night.

And wonder if the role I played,
  perhaps in some small way,
Has touched the mighty, silver giant
  I'm riding in today.

And if it did, what then of those
  young men who learned to fly,
Those boys who soon would risk their lives
  in Europe's war-torn sky?

And what of early pioneers,
  those men of daring-do,
Who, in their flimsy little craft,
  rose to the sky and flew.

Those, who at risk of life and limb,
  did brave the hostile sky,
While others said that God did not
  intend that man should fly?

All those who dared and those who died,
  assisting flying's birth,
And paved the way, that other men
  might someday leave the earth.

For life is like an endless chain,
    repeated o'er and o'er,
Where each man rises on the back
    of those who've gone before.

I sip my drink and contemplate
    the mountains down below,
With wooded slopes and rampant peaks,
    their crests all capped in snow.

And wonder if, on other worlds,
    are mountains such as these,
Where mankind may, some future day,
    fly o'er their heights with ease.

Perhaps the offspring of my sons
    may break earth's surly bond,
In spirit of adventure, bold,
    and sail the great beyond.

And in so doing, forge a link
    within that endless chain,
That had its start when first I rode
    that little, yellow plane.

Note: The little yellow planes referred to were the R.C.A.F. training
aircraft that I worked on as a mechanic during World War II.

I Saw The Soldiers Marching

I saw the soldiers marching,
one drear November day,
Those heroes bold, from wars of old,
in countries far away.

I heard the drums like thunder,
the sound of marching feet,
As men of ancient valor
marched down our little street.

I heard the skirl of bagpipes,
the blare of brasses bold,
As heroes from another time
relived the days of old.

The old, the halt, the lame, the slow,
they marched with solemn pace,
To honor comrades fallen
at another time and place.

I felt the tightness in my throat,
the tears that burned my eyes,
As I watched the quiet dignity
of old men marching by.

The fine young men, and women too,
in battles long ago,
Who gave their youth and some, their lives,
To fight our country's foe.

On this day will be remembered
by comrades who remain,
And by the heavens, weeping,
with softly falling rain.

The medals softly jingling
on every passing chest,
In memory of companions
who've long been laid to rest.

There are some unfit, and some who sit,
in wheelchairs, row on row,
While they recall what price was paid
to turn our country's foe.

And some will stand with tear-dimmed eyes,
and some with faces grim,
While all repeat the solemn vow,
"WE WILL REMEMBER THEM."

CHAPTER 2: NATURE'S TOUCH

OF NATURE, GOD AND MAN

There beside the placid waters,
   deep within a forest glade,
      I sat and sadly pondered
         'neath a mighty oak tree's shade,

On the evil wreaked on nature
   by this creature known as man,
      Who claims God bestowed dominion
         o'er the waters and the land.

Who fills the streams with poisons
   and befouls the pristine air,
      And defends his acts as "progress"
         while he strips the forests bare.

Who guts the mighty mountains
   for the riches they contain,
      And maintains that Mother Nature
         put the acid in the rain;

While his smokestacks, ever taller,
   spread a pall across the sky,
      To sear the lungs of mankind
         while fish and forests die.

Is it really true that progress
   means a car of greater speed?
      And just how many treasures
         does the average fellow need?

Should we decimate the forests
    just to advertise our wares,
        Pile the landscape high with garbage?
        And does anybody care?

If the world should end tomorrow,
    through man's excess and his greed,
        Would but one voice say, in sorrow,
        "For all this there was no need?"

Do the birds that ply the heavens,
    do the denizens of the lake,
        Do the creatures of the forest
        know that man decides their fate?

They are all creation's creatures,
    all who swim or walk or fly,
        Who are we that we may tell them
        whether they may live or die?

Then a butterfly lands on me...
    lightly as an Angel's kiss,
        And I ask myself in wonder,
        "Do I need much more than this?"

Would more money in my pocket,
    make the Sun more brightly shine?
        And would yon lake be more lovely
        if I knew 'twas truly mine?

Would the forest air be sweeter,
    were I wealthy as a king?
        Would I hear a finer music
        from the songbirds when they sing?

And the loons that laugh so loudly,
 or the beaver swimming by,
  Do they care if yonder human
   is an influential guy?

The God of all creation
 placed this bounty in our care,
  Should we leave, then, some small portion
   to our children as their share?

Or should we continue wasting
 and destroying as we go,
  'Til there's nothing left for others
   but some stumps and fields of snow?

And the waters, filled with poisons,
 are unfit for fish or man,
  Ending, in one generation,
   what has been...since time began?

Is it not now time to pay some heed
 to moderation's call,
  Before endless greed and avarice
   bring destruction to us all?

SURVIVAL

I found him 'neath a maple tree,
    just lying there on the ground,
And I saw the nest just overhead,
    from which he'd tumbled down.

I picked him up and his beak gaped wide,
    as he silently begged for food,
And my heart went out to this little stray,
    from a mother robin's brood.

For nature's way is cruel, they say,
    and only the strong survive,
And I knew if I left him lying there
    he would not reach dawn alive.

So I got my ladder and placed him back there,
    among his siblings small,
And he settled down, back in his nest,
    like he never had left at all.

But I knew ere long, as his wings grew strong,
    he would leave, as would the rest,
(Do mother birds' eyes flood o'er with tears
    when her fledglings leave the nest?)

For nature's way is hard, they say,
    still it doesn't seem quite fair,
When she's worked so hard to raise her brood,
    and once more the nest is bare.

And does the father bird worry about his young
    as he goes to sleep at night?
Does he think, sometimes, of the weakest one
    and wonder if he's all right?

Yes nature's way is hard, they say,
    and only the strong survive,
Is it best for all that the weak should fall,
    no matter how hard they strive?

Are we so enthralled by the bold and strong
    that we must ignore the meek,
When all they need is a helping hand,
    to reach the goal they seek?

If we have no time to lend a hand
    to the weaker when they fall,
The world may be a stronger place,
    but there'll be no love at all.

CASTLES IN THE SAND

The children built their castles
on the beach while tide was low,
And in all their youth and innocence
they didn't even know,

That the ocean would be rising
ere the ending of the day,
And the lapping of the water
would sweep all their work away.

Had their elders failed to tell them?
Had they failed to listen well?
Time and tide are unrelenting
as the tolling of a bell.

How the labors of a lifetime,
in indeed a single day,
By forces uncontrollable
may well be swept away.

Children watch the sands erosion,
some with laughter, some with cheers.
Some just shrug away their losses,
some console themselves with tears.

And likewise, we as adults,
if the fates should cause us pain,
Should we shrug away our losses
and proceed to build again?

Is it really worth the effort,
you may ask yourself one day,
To toil so hard for something
that the tides will sweep away?

We cannot assure our efforts,
we can't run away and hide,
And the sand's too dry for building
if we go beyond the tide.

Is it really worth the effort?
Now we hear that cry again,
Is it really worth the heartache,
all the struggle and the pain?

Should we spend our lives in striving,
like the children on the beach,
For castles unattainable
that stay beyond our reach?

If perchance we do attain them
then we find our job's not done,
We must fight now to retain them
'til our life, so short, is run.

And should we pass them to our children
as we would a piece of soil,
Will they recognize the value
of another person's toil?

All the creatures of the forest,
those that prey and those that graze,
May dine on nature's bounty
'til the ending of their days.

While man, cast in God's image,
(at least so we are told)
Must struggle ever harder
in attainment of his goal.

Did God curse man with ambition
so that peace he'd never know,
When He turned him out of Eden
on that day so long ago?

Was man's love of acquisition
but the spur that drove him on,
Fueling greed and discontentment
ever since creation's dawn?

Perhaps we should consider
as for riches great we strive,
Those who struggle not for riches
but to keep themselves alive.

And next time we're discontented
and we feel the going's rough,
We could ask ourselves this question:
"Do I not now have enough?"

CREATION

There are colors that dazzle the senses,
    and scenes that are food for the soul,
There are sounds that are sweet as God's music,
    to enjoy them you are never too old.

This morning I walked through a forest
    in riotous colors arrayed,
And I thought, "Lord, how great are your workings,"
    as I stood 'neath a tall tree that swayed.

In the breeze that blew down from the mountains,
    soft scented with odor of pine,
Bringing peace to my soul, and contentment,
    in a manner I could not define.

All touched by the hand of the Maker,
    the artist who still reigns supreme,
Displaying a random perfection,
    beyond mortal man's greatest dream.

Last winter I stood on a mountain,
    enrobed in its mantle of snow,
And I thought, "God, how great is this beauty,"
    as I gazed at the landscape below.

Where a stream wandered down through the valley,
    and a deer stood in innocent ease,
Unconcerned with the dangers about him,
    as he sampled the cool winter breeze.

Then there rose from the depths of the water,
    a muskrat, with black eyes agleam;
And their eyes met, both of them God's creatures,
    as the deer bent to drink from the stream.

And my soul slowly warmed at the picture,
    of life as the Creator planned,
And I asked, "Is there room in creation
    for that creature known simply as Man?"

Man sometimes is called, "the great builder,"
    for truly his workings are vast.
Still, God's handiwork is forever;
    the creations of man seldom last.

Great building will age and then crumble,
    for these are the workings of man,
While the mountains stand, ever unchanging,
    carved out by the Creator's hand.

Two forces forever in conflict,
　　in a struggle, unending, it seems,
Between God, who created the mountains,
　　and Man, who befouls all the streams.

A river winds through a great forest,
　　all part of the Almighty's plan,
While Man brags of how he will dam it
　　and flood countless acres of land.

Vain Man, take a leave of your boasting,
　　then turn your eyes upward and see,
The rainbow that's spanning the heavens;
　　reach out, touch the trunk of a tree.

Acknowledge the beauties of nature,
　　then perhaps, just perhaps, give a thought,
To asking the Maker's forgiveness
　　for all the destruction you've wrought.

HOMO SUPERIOR

The more I think the matter o'er
   the less I understand,
      Why God gave things to animals
      He did not give to man.

Perhaps it's not right to complain
   but really, I don't see,
      Why He gave skills to my old dog,
      He did not give to me.

My dog may not be very smart,
   but I can't take my toes,
      And roll up in a little ball
      and with them, scratch my nose.

My dog has teeth that chomp on bones
   and never seem to break,
      While my old caps keep coming off,
      each time that I eat steak.

He gave big muscles to the lion,
   the cheetah is so fleet.
      The deer, He gave four dainty hooves,
      and man got two flat feet.

He gave the birds their plumage grand,
   and speckles to the trout.
      But all he gave was hair, to man,
      and that keeps falling out.

The horse and cow may browse on grass
    that grows where'er it rains
        While man must dine at fast food joints,
          and suffer gastric pains.

The lowly frog may lie in wait
    and catch a bug for lunch.
        But there, I think I'll draw the line
          (They have a horrid crunch).

They tell me, Lord, your favorite race
    is Homo Sapien,
        Then why give such a funny face
          to poor defenseless men?

A set of teeth that scarcely bite,
    a nose that's much too small,
        A set of ears, upon the head,
          that will not move at all.

It's not that I'm ungrateful, Lord,
    forgive me if I rail,
        But why is man the only one
          who did not get a tail?

For though some folk might disagree
    I think it would be neat,
        to have a long and swinging tail
          that reaches to my feet.

With lots of fur and, on the end
   a tassel, long and wide,
      For swatting flies upon my nose
         while hands are occupied.

Perhaps a long, prehensile tail
   might be the way to go,
      One I could wrap around a branch
         while I swung to and fro.

And while we're on the subject, Lord,
   about the chimpanzee…
      He has an extra pair of hands
         as anyone can see.

To busy man, they'd be a boon,
   an aid by no means small.
      Why give them to the chimpanzee
         who does no work at all?

So Lord, if ever you decide
   to build a better man,
      Perhaps you might consider this,
         my simple little plan.

Just take the better parts of all
   and roll them into one,
      And then, why you can truly say,
         "My work is well and truly done."

WHAT I'LL LEAVE BEHIND

It's a round-trip ticket that I hold
both to and from this grand old earth,
And half of which I have cashed in
the day my mother gave me birth.

The second half I hold in trust
until that day when I must go,
Unto that spot which has no name,
that place no living soul may know.

And on the day that I depart
I know I'll leave with some regret,
There will be so much still to do,
so many jobs unfinished, yet.

I'll leave behind me no great wealth,
just several offspring, straight and strong,
And knowledge that I've done my best,
have played it square, done no man wrong.

I want no mausoleum grand,
nor seal my ashes in an urn,
For I was formed from dust of earth
and to that earth I must return.

But if you would, cremate my bones,
then cast my ashes on the breeze,
That they may land on field and streams
and some may lodge among the trees.

And that which lands on waters, swift,
must someday reach the rolling sea.
But always, upon God's green earth,
there will remain a part of me.

The product of my time on earth
may not be great, as such are weighed,
I only know I did my best,
will face my Maker, unafraid.

And if my epitaph you write,
I wish no eulogy so grand.
But if, perhaps, you spare a line,
then let it read, "Here was a man."

CHAPTER 3: DOWN A COUNTRY LANE

THE BROOK

You asked for a story so I'll spin you a yarn
About a small brook that ran back of the barn.
Where the bullfrogs were large and the minnows swam free,
And when I was a kid it belonged just to me.

The stream was quite shallow except for one pool
That was shaped like a basin, where the water ran cool,
Lying there in the shadow of a big maple's shade,
Where butterflies fluttered and dragonflies played.

There were chub, there were shiners,
there were little brown trout,
In the bottom were crawfish who scuttled about,
Like miniature lobsters, bent on some scheme,
As they scavenged for food in the crystal clear stream.

There were newts for the catching, for any who dared,
There were bulgy-eyed frogs that just floated and stared.
And a slow, solemn turtle who lived quite alone,
Near the edge of the bank, 'neath a big, sloping stone.

Ah, the hours I spent wading barefoot, in that brook,
And fishing for trout with a worm and a hook.
And the pool where I bathed, with my best buddy, Jim,
Until the day that a garter snake slipped in to swim.

And we both left the pool and sat down on a log
While we watched that small garter snake stalking a frog.
Then Jimmy decided, "Aw, for goodness sake,
Let's go on back in, that's an awful small snake."

We built us a hut that was meant just for two
At the bend in the stream where the willow shrubs grew.
And we slept there at night, with a robe for a bed,
While a hoot owl made weird, spooky sounds overhead.

And fireflies did their darndest to light up the gloom,
While we lay there, half-scared, in our snug little room.
Yes, we played by that stream by night and by day,
And we sure learned a lot about nature that way.

But small boys grow up and, too quickly it seems,
They forget about pools and small rippling streams.
But the brook waits there patiently hoping some day,
Some other small kids will come by there to play.

FRESH WATER FROM THE SPRING

When I was young I bought a farm
    from a guy named Jim McFee,
        He hadn't any sons,
            that's why he sold the farm to me.

There was a swamp down at the north end,
    at the south there was a wood,
        While the land between was stony,
            still, the water sure was good.

'Cause a spring up in the south end
    bubbled up from 'neath the ground,
        It was icy cold in summer
            and it flowed the year around.

So I ran a pipe down from it
    and I brought it to the house,
        To a tap right in the kitchen
            and that sure did please my spouse.

For those were the 'Dirty Thirties'
    and the living was real hard,
        And darn near all our neighbors
            had a well out in the yard.

Where they got their drinking water,
    and to bathe, (for those who did),
        And to do the family washing,
            which was tough if you had kids.

Guess maybe I was kind of smug
　　as I bragged of what I'd done,
　　　　Still, it surely was a comfort
　　　　　　just to watch that faucet run.

While thinking how those city folk
　　drank water from a river,
　　　　That folk upstream dumped sewage in,
　　　　　　the thought just made me shiver.

Well I knew the stuff I drank was clean
　　and I sure knew it was good,
　　　　As it flowed down from that little spring
　　　　　　away up in the wood.

'Cause I'd built a barbed wire fence around
　　to keep the cattle out,
　　　　And I'd put a cover on it,
　　　　　　it was clean, I had no doubt.

Then one day my wife remarked
　　it didn't run the way it should,
　　　　Took too long to fill a bucket,
　　　　　　now that really wasn't good.

So I told my wife, "I'll fix it,"
　　but a couple weeks went by,
　　　　And then, on a Sunday morning,
　　　　　　why that doggone tap went dry.

So I told my wife that I would go
　　and fix it, if I could,
　　　　And then I rounded up some tools
　　　　　　and I headed for the wood.

Well the cover was still on it,
    resting on a base of poles,
        But some hunter, with a shotgun,
            had plumb riddled it with holes.

Big enough to put your foot through,
    if a man felt so inclined,
        And I looked at all that damage,
            kind of worried what I'd find.

Then I lifted up the cover,
    scared I'd find the thing was dry,
        But the spring inside was brim-full…
            and then something caught my eye.

In a corner of the spring hole,
    'bout a couple of feet down,
        There was something, black and hairy,
            that had tumbled in and drowned.

Though 'twas getting kinda rotten,
    I could tell it was a skunk,
        By the white stripes down its backbone
            and the way the sucker stunk.

It was bloated and disgusting
    and, oh brother! it was ripe,
        And its backside had got stuck into
            the water intake pipe.

Well, I cut a stick to fish it out,
    there was nothing else to do,
        And it was then I lost my breakfast,
            think I lost my supper too.

As I thought of all that water
  I had drunk in days gone by,
    And how I'd bragged to all my friends,
      it made me want to cry.

Since it happened on a Sunday,
  I suppose as like as not,
    The Lord did it to punish me
      for boasting such a lot.

An' I guess I said some nasty words
  as I stood there in the sun,
    But it didn't help a bit to curse
      that hunter and his gun.

So I went and washed my mouth out
  with some water from the creek,
    And I got our drinking water
      from our neighbor, for a week.

I never told my wife the truth
  'cause I knew she'd have a fit,
    But every time I think of it,
      it makes me want to spit.

JAKE AND THE DUCKS

Jake Lewis is a farmer
and a long-time friend of mine,
Owns a couple hundred acres
down along the county line.

Now old Jake he likes his hunting
and I know that every Fall,
When the leaves start changing colors,
why ol' Jake will give a call.

Now I don't care much for hunting
and I've said as much to Jake,
In the hope he'll get discouraged,
but it never seems to take.

Last week again it happened,
Jake, he called me on the phone,
And said, "Drop around on Sunday,
I don't like to hunt alone."

"It's the first day of the season,
we can bag a duck or two,
There's some big, fat, sassy mallards
been a'hanging 'round the slough."

I told Jake I'd loaned my shotgun
and I hadn't got it back,
But Jake said not to worry,
he'd a spare one on the rack.

Since I had no more excuses,
I gave up and said, "All right."
Jake said, "Good! Just get here early,
we can start before daylight."

Jake was ready when I got there
and he said, "This should be fun,
It's a perfect day for hunting,
but you gotta have a gun."

When he took it off the gun rack,
first I thought it was a joke,
It was a big old Ivor Johnson,
double barrel'd, with open choke.

It was ancient, it was heavy
and a mighty sturdy tool,
And its two big outside hammers
looked like ears upon a mule.

Jake said, "Now I gotta warn you,
it's a twelve gauge, kicks like Hell,"
Then he opened up a cupboard
and he handed me some shells.

Well we set off for the back lot,
me in the lead, then Jake,
While his big old hound-dog, Rufus,
came a trailing in our wake.

It was a short walk to the back lot
and we got there before dawn,
We could hear the mallards talking
to each other on the pond.

As the sun tipped the horizon
just one single duck took flight,
Jake got off a shot but missed him,
then I got him in my sight.

But that doggone dog was gun shy
and he headed for the trees,
Hit me just as I was aiming,
got me right behind the knees.

I had fingers on both triggers
and I pulled them as I fell,
And a double load of buckshot
tore that mallard all to hell.

I went sailing over backwards
and I landed with a thud,
From my shoulders to my backside,
I was inches deep in mud.

Jake, who hadn't seen the dog take off,
was laughing like a nut,
He was sure it was the shotgun
that had knocked me on my butt.

We retrieved some skin and feathers
that were scattered on the ground,
There was not another mallard,
I am sure, for miles around.

I started in to cussing then,
and when I turned to Jake,
He said, "Sorry, guess I gave you
the wrong ammo by mistake."

Well, we went home empty handed
and Jake's wife said not a word,
She just fried us up some pork chops,
served with dressing for a bird.

The old dog he was lying
just beside the kitchen door,
Casting nervous glances at me;
guess he knew that I was sore.

But the next time Jake goes hunting,
I will swear upon my oath,
He can take me or take the dog;
he sure ain't taking both.

THE HUNTER

The hunter sat on a rotted log,
    on his face was a pensive frown;
        Three times today he had crossed the spoor,
        now the sun was going down.

The deer had only his native stealth,
    while he had a high-powered gun,
        And yet, he reflected, the deer was ahead,
        on a score of three to one.

He pondered awhile, then made up his mind,
    he would stay in the woods that night,
        Then without fail, he would pick up the trail
        with the early morning light.

A lunch was packed in his haversack
    and he'd drink from nearby stream,
        While the moss covered knoll would be his bed,
        as he lay down that night to dream.

With dry moss and twigs, then bits of wood,
    he laid him a fire with care,
        'Twas a matter of pride, one match must do,
        he had only a few to spare.

He reached for a pebble to light his match,
    but found in his hand instead,
        A bit of a flint, grown o'er with moss,
        in the shape of an arrowhead.

He struck a light, the fire flared up,
    then he gazed at the flint once more,
        This artifact carved by a man long dead,
            from a culture and time of yore.

The hunter fondled the arrowhead,
    as he gazed in the campfire's light,
        And the flickering flames formed pictures strange,
            as he stared in their depths that night.

In contemplation he watched the flames
    'til his eyelids closed in sleep,
        And the sounds of night were his lullaby,
            alone in the forest deep.

And he thought, as he lay down by the fire,
    in a mood approaching bliss,
        When the stomach is full and the body warm,
            what man needs more than this?

Curled by the fire, the hunter lay;
    the arrowhead in his hand,
        But the dreams that haunted his sleep that night,
            weren't those of a modern man.

For the world of today had slipped away
    and he was a warrior, instead,
        Who stalked the deer with a bow and spear
            and a flint-tipped arrowhead.

And his moccasin'd feet trod silently,
    as he crossed the forest floor,
        For he knew that he was hunted too,
            as he followed a fresh-laid spoor.

In the chill of dawn the hunter rose,
    to the early morning's light,
        And his mind was filled with the images
            that had haunted his dreams last night.

He walked to the stream to have a drink
    and there, in the weeds and muck,
        As plain as bold as tho' carved in stone,
            were the tracks of a full-grown buck.

The deer, in the night, had doubled back,
    not fearing his stalker's gun,
        And the man reflected, while standing there,
            how hunter and prey were one.

For he realized that, as he lay
    enwrapped in his dreams so deep,
        The deer who had found him in the night,
            could have gored him in his sleep.

He pondered, had their roles been changed,
    would he have turned away,
        And simply left the stag to rest,
            to challenge another day?

Then came a thought to give him pause,
   as he stood with bated breath,
      What to a hunter was merely sport,
        to a deer was life and death.

The deer, today, would do what he must,
   for his was the life at stake,
      While he, the man, was in command
        and he had a choice to make.

Behind him lay civilization's path,
   before him a fresh-laid spoor,
      But the hunter knew in his heart of hearts
        that this day he would hunt no more.

Then he reached for his compass to guide him home
   and found in his hand, instead,
      A piece of flint, o'er grown with moss,
        in the shape of an arrowhead.

THE CELEBRATION

Our home in the country was built at a time
when living conditions were hard,
A pump supplied water, a stove gave you heat
and the privy was in the backyard.

When we bought the house, we were rugged and young
and we took all those things in our stride,
But after one Winter, a plumber was called
to construct us a bathroom, inside.

Our wee, vine-covered biffy was never torn down
but was left as an object of fun,
However, 'ere long 'twas apparent to all
it had found its own place in the sun.

It provided, for one thing, a cozy retreat
from the toil and the turmoil of life,
Where one could retire with the current Esquire
and escape from the voice of the wife.

Our bathroom, alas, was not in its class
for one thing, the walls were too thin,
You no sooner sat down with a good book in hand
than the children would yell to get in.

So the privy outside was my joy and my pride
and for many a long year it stood,
While the bees built a nest and the flies buzzed with zest,
and the termites, they gnawed at the wood.

And the roof sprung a leak and the hinges did squeak
and the floor, it did sag 'neath my feet;
While I thought, with some sorrow, of tearing it down;
then one day my dear wife said, "Sweet,

You know that I'm not the sort of a wife
who needlessly raises a fuss,
But that shack in the backyard has just got to go
for our neighbors are laughing at us."

"If you'll just tear it down and then level the ground
we can plant us a bush or a vine."
Then our youngest lad snickered, "That's one place I'll bet
that most anything would grow fine."

Now the date of the founding of our little Town
is a date of which we are all proud.
In fact, it's the only darn day of the year
when bonfires are ever allowed.

So the children and I decided that night
that with Founder's Day coming around,
To observe it, we'd have a big fire of our own
and burn that old shack to the ground.

Well, my wife was disgusted, said she wanted no part
('course women are funny that way),
But the kids and I bought some wieners and drinks
and sorted out records to play.

We lit it at dusk and the wood was so dry
it flared up like grease on a griddle,
While a cloud of black smoke from the tar-papered roof
divided our Town down the middle.

'Tween the smoke and the flames, it wasn't too long
'til the firemen came calling around;
But the fire chief just said, "Keep it under control,
you've by far the best bonfire in town."

On the street behind ours lived a woman alone,
a lady named Mrs. O'Hare,
Who had left her wash out on the line overnight
as she said, "To give it some air."

But a shift in the wind brought a cloud of smoke down
to sully both clothing and sheet,
And the language I heard from Mrs. O'Hare,
I am certain I'll never repeat.

Now a few days before, quite unknown to me,
the children, some fireworks had gotten,
Which they'd stored in the privy to set off that night;
and then, had completely forgotten.

My first indication that things were not right
was when rockets, bright, took to the air;
While my patio awning was then set alight
by something that looked like a flare.

Now the high-leaping flames, still under control,
    attracted some folk to the scene,
And they stood 'round the fire, to watch and admire
    the flames of pink, yellow and green.

Then an engineer said, "Those colors are caused
    by iron rust and metal corrosion."
And 'twas right at this point that our poor little shack
    went up in a massive explosion.

As the debris rained down over half of the town,
    my neighbor, old Mr. McKenna,
Phoned to ask if I'd please take my toilet seat down
    from the top of his T.V. antenna.

My neighbor next door said, "I'm glad you weren't hurt,"
    then he laughed 'til he bent over double,
And the lesson I've learned is that things you don't know
    quite often can get you in trouble.

THIS PIECE OF EARTH

It is not really much, as such things go,
Just a run-down farm on a county line,
And nobody envies me, I know,
This wee bit of earth that I call mine.

The hay is patchy, the soil is thin,
Still, the weeds and the sage brush grow just fine,
And part of the barn has fallen in,
On this little place that I call mine.

The bank owns most of my city home,
And to buy my car I needed a loan,
And I'm still making payments on the stove and fridge,
But this little place is mine alone.

The man that I am, grew from this soil,
For this is the spot I once called home.
The product of father and grandad's toil,
This one piece of earth I can call my own.

The old farmhouse is vacant now,
Its gaping door a toothless grin,
But I still remember my childhood days
And all of the love that dwelt within.

I still can see, in memory's eye,
The little creek where I built a bridge,
The vines and briars that bore their fruit,
The solemn pines atop the ridge.

There was everything there that a child might wish,
From scented hayfield to forest, cool,
Where a boy might retire to dream his dreams,
Or swim with the fish in a sunlit pool.

'Twas hard enough, God knows it's true,
To sustain ourselves on that skimpy soil,
But we made our living as poor folks must,
With muscles and sweat and endless toil

Accepting the tasks that were our lot,
In freezing cold or the blazing sun,
A boy who sought the meaning of life,
Two parents whose labors were never done.

It's very hard to explain today,
I am certain my children don't understand,
The attachment I feel for this bit of earth,
This worn out, run down piece of land.

But 'twas all that my father bequeathed to me,
This sum of a lifetime's work and toil,
How could I, then, betray his trust
And sell to another, this piece of soil?

I sense his presence all about,
By shaded stream or on wooded hill,
And still recall the things he taught,
His wisdom and council guide me still.

So when I want to regain my soul,
I come back here, where it all began,
For I know that the values that guide my life
Were learned in my youth, on this piece of land.

CHAPTER 4: OUR NEIGHBORS

CHARLEY BAKER'S FUNERAL

Now old Charley Baker, as everyone knew,
was a mean and cantankerous old cuss.
Never known to smile, he was easily riled,
ever ready to fume and to fuss.

No one really liked him, even guys from his youth
who had known the man all his life;
It was plain to be seen he was just rotten mean
and everyone pitied his wife.

He seldom was heard to say a kind word
and always was primed for a fight,
He was rude, he was crude and I am certain he sued
just about every neighbor in sight.

There was no use in trying to be Charley's friend
and, truthfully nobody tried;
And that's why it's so strange what occurred at the end
when we heard that old Charley had died.

They found him sprawled out on the horse stable floor
with a filthy old cap on his head,
There he lay, small and sad, in the muck and manure
for old Charley Baker was dead.

Now here was a man whom no one could stand,
who'd been cussed and reviled all his life,
But the newspaper said, "Charley Baker is dead,
he'll be mourned by two sons and his wife."

Mrs. Riley, who'd fought with old Charley for years
and had once put a curse on his head,
Attended the mourning and shed copious tears
because old Charley Baker was dead.

And his wife showed her grief (or perhaps 'twas relief)
as she sat there so dry-eyed and prim,
While the banker dropped 'round and in tones so profound
said, "Life won't be the same without him."

Then Eddy McHame, a close neighbor, came
and said, as he wiped away tears,
"He was a nice guy," which was a poor try
'cause they hadn't spoken in years.

When the Reverend arrived he said a short prayer
and the funeral arrangements were planned,
When they asked for pallbearers the hands all went up,
yes, they all volunteered, to a man.

The day of the funeral the folks all turned out,
the Church, to the doorway, was packed,
And I heard someone murmur, "They're here to make sure
that the old devil's not coming back."

Then the minister spoke and it was a sad joke,
though I feel that the man was sincere,
For he never once mentioned what everyone knew,
Charley Baker had called him a "Queer."

Then they picked up the coffin, three men to a side
and they walked with a pace sad and slow,
And I couldn't help thinking Charley had the last laugh,
'cause he owed every one of them dough.

So it seems for a guy who was such a mean cuss in life
that it turned out all right in the end,
And I couldn't believe, as I told my good wife,
Charley Baker had so many friends.

EDUCATED EDDY

Eddy Jackson was a burglar
   and he was a pleasant lad,
Quite skilled in his profession,
   'til the night his luck turned bad.

You see Eddy had a problem;
   he could neither read nor write.
And that's the reason he got caught
   while at his work one night.

He had burglarized a mansion
   and had made a decent score,
But Eddy couldn't read the sign
   that was posted on the door.

Seemed this house had security,
   with the firm of Stern and Freed,
But Eddy didn't know this,
   because Eddy couldn't read.

He left there quite elated
   for the job, he felt, was neat,
'Til he met four big policemen
   who'd been waiting in the street.

Now the judge was not too friendly
   and much to Ed's chagrin
Gave him three years in the slammer
   to repent for all his sins.

But the warden showed compassion
    for in his career he'd found,
That with help and understanding
    some crooks could be turned around.

He felt sympathy for Eddy,
    for he recognized his need,
And enrolled him with a tutor
    so that Ed could learn to read.

As young ducklings take to water
    and as piglets take to swill,
Eddy Jackson took to learning,
    seems he couldn't get his fill.

Read the total works of Shakespeare,
    could quote Kipling by the ream,
To become a learned person
    was his object and his dream.

Other cons found it amusing,
    some did snicker, some did chide,
Called him "Educated Eddy"
    but he bore the name with pride.

Read the works of Scott and Thoreau,
    read *The Rise and Fall of Rome*,
Because Educated Eddy
    cherished every type of tome.

Then came the break for which most cons
    would sell their very soul;
Eight months off for good behavior,
    Eddy Jackson made parole.

Eddy vowed, "From this day forward
    I will be an honest man,
Thank you, Sir, for all your kindness,"
    then he shook the Warden's hand.

And the Warden beamed with pleasure
    as young Ed walked through the door,
He'd reformed another felon;
    this young man would steal no more.

Three months passed and nothing happened,
    three months passed and all was right,
No one heard from Eddy Jackson,
    seemed he'd just dropped out of sight.

Then one day a wealthy oilman
    realized, to his chagrin,
That his home, he'd thought protected,
    had somehow been broken in.

Eddy Jackson'd found a textbook
    telling all about alarms,
Giving plans and the instructions,
    how to build them, or disarm.

Seems our hero, Eddy Jackson,
    now could enter homes with ease,
Alarms, to him, were no deterrent,
    as for locks, they were a breeze.

And so Eddy broke and entered,
    cased the house, to his dismay,
He found very little in it
    he would care to tote away.

Though the walls were lined with paintings,
    most were much too large to haul,
And Jackson found he could not crack
    the safe set in the wall.

But within a flimsy showcase,
        Ed could not believe his luck,
Sat a rare and ancient manuscript
        worth several million bucks.

Somewhere on a distant island,
        'neath the Caribbean sun,
Lives a guy named Eddy Jackson,
        he's retired, his work is done.

He pursues his favorite hobby,
        reading books by famous men,
One big score was all he needed,
        he need never work again.

Moves in all the proper circles,
        popular fellow about town;
Uses grammar quite exquisite
        and his knowledge seems profound.

No one knows his sordid background,
        Ed is living like a king,
And he'll tell you education
        is a truly wondrous thing.

PURE SPECULATION

Now Jim Brown had twisted his ankle,
    it was swollen and causing him pain,
        When Mrs. O'Reilly saw him that day
           he was limping and using a cane.

Though she wasn't really a gossip,
    she felt that she just had to tell,
        So she phoned her best friend, Alice Berney,
           and she said, "Poor old Jim's not too well."

"I saw him today at the market,
    and he seemed in such terrible pain,
        He was moving quite slow, like an old man, you know,
           and he even was using a cane."

Mrs. Berney, she listened with interest
    (she hadn't too much else to do),
        Then she phoned an old friend at the lawn bowling club
           to learn if the story was true.

Well down at the club, Billy Horton,
    admitted that he hadn't heard,
        But he did know Jim hadn't been bowling,
           perhaps he should pass on the word.

Tom Gibbs at Canadian Legion,
    said, "It don't surprise me at all;
        I knew when he bought that fool ten speed,
           that sooner or later he'd fall."

"It sounds, by the way you describe it,
    like he had a serious slip,
        You say that he's walking with crutches?
           He's probably fractured his hip."

He told all that night at the meeting,
   while admitting he knew few details,
      Then someone suggested, "Jim probably fell
      on one of those cycling trails."

Next day, the tale was Jim had fallen,
   and landed on top of his head,
      What started out as a sprained ankle
      had some folks convinced he was dead.

By now Jimmy's wife was near frantic,
   the phone had been ringing for hours,
      And the fellows down there at the Legion
      had chipped in to send him some flowers.

Some friends called to offer condolence
   and that night Father Fagen dropped in,
      But he found Jim in excellent spirits;
      in fact, he was drinking a gin.

He offered a drink to the Padré,
   who replied, "Sure, I'll have one, with lime,
      I had come, Jim, to give you absolution,
      but I see I'd be wasting my time."

So they sat and they had several tall ones,
   even joined in an old Irish song,
      Then the priest said, "I don't mean to scold, Jim,
      but I hope you realize you did wrong."

"For it's really not right to start rumors
   and frighten your neighbors this way,
      For your penance let's finish this bottle,
      and then I must be on my way."

OLD RUFE

I first met old Rufe when I was a boy,
a kid on his very first job.
Now Rufe was a bachelor, addicted to drink,
uncouth and a bit of a slob.

He was bowlegged and small but 'wang' leather tough
and he worked me near into the earth,
While he made snide remarks in his whiskey-rough voice
'til I hated the day of his birth.

Yes, I was a boy but he made me a man
for his razzing did give me a push,
And he taught me the things that I needed to know,
about how to survive in the bush.

By the end of the winter my hate was all gone
for I finally did understand,
Though he was uncouth with an axe or a saw
he sure was one hell of a man.

Then one day he said I was holding my own
and did pretty good work, now and then,
And I realized with joy I was no more a boy
but an adult, a man among men.

And then the War came and I went to sign up
and Rufus he said, "Well, that's grand,
But there's only one problem, now I've got to find
and break in another good man."

Then he went to the cupboard and took out a jug
and he said, "Do you know what I think?
If you're man enough to go out there and fight,
you're sure big enough for a drink."

So he poured us two drinks that were generous indeed
and we talked until late in the night,
And I found my way home 'neath the cold winter moon
with a head that was fuzzy and light.

On the day that I left I said my "good-byes,"
little knowing if I would be back,
As the bus rolled away I saw Rufus wave,
from the door of his clapboard shack.

When the Drill Sergeant yelled, "You're all snotty nosed kids
and I'm going to make men out of you,"
I smiled to myself, because after old Rufe,
there wasn't much more he could do.

So I ran and I climbed and did close order drill
and I marched in a line every day.
But after the winters I'd spent in the woods,
this wasn't hard work, it was play!

And though the War took several years of my life,
I was lucky and came to no harm,
And when it was over I turned in my gear,
but I didn't go back to the farm.

Well I didn't see Rufe for many a year,
for the City was so far away,
But I promised myself that if I came near
I would drop in and see him one day.

When he came to the door I could see at a glance
that the whiskey was taking its toll,
He was weathered and bent as the stem of his pipe
and God, he looked wizened and old.

But he stuck out his hand and he placed it in mine
and he said, "Hey, I'm glad you could come,
The boy just delivered a fresh case of beer,
come on in and help me drink some."

So we sat and drank beer and we talked of old times
and I promised that I would return,
But I never got back to see him again,
'twas about a year later I learned,

Rufe had gone to the Doctor, said, "I'm near eighty-two
and I've always been healthy and well,
But I think that I've picked up a bit of the 'flu
because lately I'm feeling like hell."

The Doc checked him out and then said with a frown
"Well, Rufus, I have some bad news,
Your liver is shot and you're going to cash in,
unless you lay off the booze."

Rufus said, "I've no wife and I've drank all my life,
if I'm going, I'll go like a Man,
If I've got to cash in then I'll do it in style
with a bottle of Scotch in my hand."

Then he called all his friends, said, "I've been to the Doc
and he tells me the end is quite near,
But before a man dies he should say his good-byes;
How about coming around for a beer?"

I'm told that the party went on several days
and that Rufus he picked up the bill,
And they drank to his health and to his future wealth,
although they all knew he was ill.

'Twas several weeks later Rufe cashed in his chips,
one evening a neighbor dropped in,
Found him dead on the floor with a smile on his puss,
on the table a bottle of gin.

There's some good folk say that Rufe was a bum,
a ruffian, a man of no worth,
But I happen to know that, like others before,
old Rufe left his mark on this earth.

Hope God in his wisdom provided a place
where old Rufe and his raffish old friends,
Can sit, smoke their pipes, tell each other lies
and perhaps, have a beer now and then.

For I happen to feel that there's good in all men
and if ever I'm needful of proof,
I'll hearken once more to the days of my youth
and the life and the times of old Rufe.

THE BALLAD OF BOBBY O'DELL

I remember the first time, 'twas down on the Strip
in a joint known as "Willie's Café."
A clean-cut young fellow with a great, big guitar
and a smile that would light up your day.

Just a-sittin' up there on a two-by-four stage
with a microphone, next to the bar,
And he smiled at the gang, who were sipping their booze,
then he started to play his guitar.

Yeah, he played a few chords then he started to sing,
oh Lord! His voice rang like a bell,
And when folks stopped applauding, he flashed that big smile
and said "Hi! Folks, I'm Bobby O'Dell."

He reminded me then of when I was a youth,
and fancied myself as a star;
And how, when I learned of the dues I must pay,
I had simply hung up my guitar.

I remembered so well all those smoky old bars
where I'd played for tips, sometimes for free,
While the drinkers applauded and sent me up beers;
for a moment young Bobby was me.

I thought as I sat there, this kid had it all;
he had stage presence, talent and charm.
And for two hours he held that crowd in his hand,
then he left, with a girl on his arm.

I saw them drive off, with the girl at the wheel,
in a Mustang of bright apple green;
And I thought to myself, this was sure heady stuff,
for a kid who was barely nineteen.

Now I'm not a fellow who hangs around bars,
but I dropped in next night for a while,
And there was young Bobby with his great big guitar,
his songs and his high-voltage smile.

The word had gone out, he was packing them in,
he had talent, that much I could tell,
And I wondered that night what the future might hold
for a youngster named Bobby O'Dell.

Then one night I dropped in and the stage it was bare,
and the waiter said Bobby had gone.
He'd been hired by a big club just outside of town,
Yes! Bobby was moving right on.

It seemed for a while he just couldn't go wrong,
his star just continued to rise.
And the girl with the Mustang kept tagging along,
we could all see the love in her eyes.

Then he picked up a group and he went on a tour,
and for seven months they were apart;
When he came back, the girl with the Mustang was gone,
and I know it broke young Bobby's heart.

But wherever there's glamour you'll always find girls,
and whenever a guy's on a roll,
He'll always have friends to drink up his booze,
and to help him to spend all his gold.

Yes! We all thought Bobby, for stardom was bound,
and he thought the same thing, because,
His fair-weather buddies kept hanging around,
to tell him how great that he was.

But the years rolled along and we never did hear
a hit song by Bobby O'Dell,
And the girls came and went and his money was spent
making records that just didn't sell.

Well some folks get rich and others stay poor,
and no one's quite sure what it takes.
But hard work and trying are never enough,
unless a guy gets a few breaks.

For years he played "lead-on" for recording stars,
whose talent was less than his own,
And in between, played in the nightclubs and bars,
while Lady Luck left him alone.

It's been a rough row, for Bobby, I know,
doing night clubs for twenty-one years,
He's a rasp in his voice from the whiskey and smoke,
and a belly from too many beers.

The lines in his face look etched into place,
and there's gray in the hair on his head,
And he doesn't look forty, he looks fifty-five,
from the life that the poor guy has led.

He's playing these days at a joint known as "Jiggs"
and I hear he's not doing too well.
The young guys are picking up all the good gigs,
who remembers this guy named O'Dell?

He still has his buddies, they're hanging around,
to pick up whatever is free;
But they can't help a fellow who's on his way down,
'cause they're just a hard up as he.

Oh, he can still charm the birds out of the trees,
and sing like an angel, it seems,
But now it looks like he's just putting in time,
as though he has lost all his dreams.

I should have tried harder to steer Bobby right,
but I didn't, that's why I feel bad.
But would he have listened or gone his own way -
whoever pays heed to his Dad?

JEREMY BROWN

Not every man can achieve success,
    a fella can only try,
        But a man is a man if he does his best
          An' don't cheat the other guy.

Yes this is the way it was told to me
    by a man named Jeremy Brown,
        Who owned a scrubby old run-down farm
          a few miles outside of Town.

There was no doubt at all that Jerry was poor,
    for he worked on that farm alone,
        Since his wife had run off, many years before,
          with a fellow named Tim Malone.

And I don't know where his kids had gone,
    I just know they weren't around.
        Guess none of 'em wanted that run-down farm
          that was home to Jeremy Brown.

His barn was old and it tilted a bit,
    and we knew that inside it housed
        A big gray team, a couple of goats,
          and a dozen milking cows.

And he worked his farm as a farmer must,
    from dawn 'til the sun went down,
        As he made his living, one man alone,
          and we all liked Jeremy Brown.

There were some who said he was seldom in Church
and wasn't a Christian man,
Yet we all knew he was always there
when someone could use a hand.

And the old farmhouse was a 'hangout' spot
for half of the boys in Town,
We were always sure of a welcome there
at the home of Jeremy Brown.

He always knew if we wanted to talk,
or wanted to be alone,
And we spoke of things, to Jeremy Brown,
that we couldn't discuss at home.

But the years passed by for Jeremy Brown
and his hair turned a silver-gray,
And most of the boys who had hung around,
had grown up and moved away.

And the kids who were his neither came nor wrote,
then one day the Preacher said,
"Mr. Brown, you're a man alone,
who will bury you when you're dead?"

Well! Jeremy, he just thought awhile,
then he laughed and said, "What the hell!
If my neighbors don't bury me for love,
they will when I start to smell!"

And then one day there was no milk out
    when the creamery truck came 'long,
        And the dog was crying outside the door,
            for old Jeremy Brown was gone.

They found him there, with his pipe in hand,
    stretched out on his rumpled bed,
        A peaceful smile on his wrinkled face
            and a Bible beside his head.

The funeral procession stretched out for miles
    on a sunny August day,
        For the boys he'd befriended all were there,
            some coming from miles away.

His neighbors, of course, were there as well;
    there was more than one tear-stained face,
        As we carried our old friend, Jeremy Brown,
            to his final resting place.

He had worked so hard for so many years,
    to some it did not seem fair
        That all he had left was a rundown farm
            and some children who didn't care.

But I thought as I looked down the road that day,
    at that funeral so long and grand,
        Jerry may have been poor, but in ways that count,
            he was a SUCCESSFUL man.

Chapter 5: *Musings*

Chance

There are very few things in the life of a man
that ever turn out the way they're planned.
You try real hard and you place your trust,
then you watch the whole darn thing go bust.
But you pick yourself up, you give a grin,
you dust yourself off and you try again.

There isn't much use in lying there
and telling yourself that life's unfair.
If life were fair, consider this fact:
we'd all be driving a Cadillac.
At the goodies of life, we'd have our turn,
and all of us would have money to burn.

If life were fair, of this I'm sure,
there would be no rich, there would be no poor.
There would be no short, there would be no tall,
and no one would have to work at all.
But the cold, hard facts of life, my friend,
are that life's not fair and it never has been.

So you have a choice, you can get up and try,
or lie there and blame the other guy.
If you think real hard you'll realize it's true,
the guy who's to blame for your luck – is you!
And forget the fact that life's not fair,
for the whole truth is…most folks don't care.

I, CAMERA

I've no voice, no soul and no conscience
Just a thing made of metal and glass,
But ah! in the hands of a master
I can show you both present and past.

I have seen both the failures and triumphs
Been there for a baby's first cry,
Recorded the tears and the anguish
When a great airship fell from the sky.

I have shown you the face of your forebears
And scenes that are long in the past,
You've guessed it – that's right, I'm a Camera,
Just a thing made of metal and glass.

I have shown you things of great beauty
And brought home the horrors of War,
I have plunged to the depths on the ocean
And recorded things ne'er seen before.

I have seen both the fair and the ugly,
Both the evil and goodness of life;
The wonder of mankind's creations,
The destruction that stems from his strife.

A lovely young girl of high fashion,
A woman who's wizened and old,
In each, I've seen beauty surpassing
The beauty of diamonds or gold.

As a fine horse has need of a rider
    Or a racecar, a driver of skill,
        I too need the skills of my master,
            My purpose in life to fulfill.

In his hands I'm creator of magic
    Though I've never been known to lie,
        I sometimes enhance and embroider,
            (Did I say he's a talented guy?)

Too often he goes unrewarded
    (For men love the thing that is free)
        As he shows them a world all around them
            They otherwise, never would see.

He may well be a man known to science
    Or an artist, as mad as a loon,
        Or a man of adventure who takes me
            When he goes for a stroll on the moon.

And our work will be ever enduring
    While other works, greater, will pass.
        But then, I am only a Camera,
            Just a thing made of metal and glass.

NIGHT RUN

The windshield wipers click in time
as they swing across their arc,
And the headlamps, bright, push back the night
as they cleave the rain-swept dark.

There's wet macadam beneath my wheels
and a ribbon of black ahead,
Where oxen at one time pulled their carts
with slow and stately tread.

Off to my right there's a glow of light
from a farmhouse by a wood,
While just beyond there's a factory, grand,
where at one time a teepee stood.

I follow a trail that once was trod
by hunters and trappers bold,
And earlier still, was probably made
by bronze-skinned men of old.

In the whisper of tires on the rain-slicked road,
I can hear their silent tread,
As I point the nose of my steed of steel
toward home, so far ahead.

I think with longing, of home and bed,
some three hundred miles away,
And my eyelids droop and I shake my head,
for my mind has begun to stray.

I guess fatigue has clouded my brain,
for off to the right I see,
A big canoe filled with voyageurs,
and they're keeping pace with me.

And just beyond that bend in the road
I see a lambent glow,
There are teepees there, of that I'll swear,
and campfires burning low.

While just beyond, an old log fort
and uniforms so bright,
As sentries walk their lonely paths
and keep their watch by night.

Imagination run amok?
Or is it the dark and rain?
All I know is that scenes of the past
keep running through my brain.

Coureur de bois, who trapped their furs
and walked the timbered tract,
And craggy men who turned the soil
and pushed the forest back.

Soldiers of old, who shed their blood
to claim the virgin land,
And give us what we have today,
a country so strong and grand.

And now I can see a glow of lights,
there's a trucker's stop ahead,
Guess I should stop and have a bite
and some coffee to clear my head.

I need to be sharp, for the road ahead
is dark and slick with rain,
And I can't drive while ghosts, long dead,
keep running through my brain.

THE FINAL FOLLY

When from the loneliness of space
  the Lord reached out a mighty hand,
    And fashioned He a living thing,
      composed of water, air and land.
        And on the earth life grew apace,
          from mighty trees to grassy deep;
            Upon the prairies, rolling, wide,
              in valleys and on mountains steep.

'Twas then he filled the earth with life,
  all things that fly or walk or crawl,
    All things that swim beneath the sea,
      from dinosaurs to insects small.
        Then God looked down upon his earth
          and all worked well, as he had planned,
            And introduced one final piece,
              a weakling thing, a thing called "Man."

And then God pondered for a space,
  for in a world where all must strive
    For food, for shelter, for a mate,
      was man too feeble to survive?
        No teeth to rend, no hooves to kick,
          no horns to pierce nor speed to run,
            God said, "You're foremost in my plan
              so you must have a brain, my son."

To feeble man he gave a brain,
  a brain to scheme, a brain to plan;
    Then said, "Whatever shall transpire,
      the lords of earth shall be called Man."
        So Man walked forth upon the earth
          and, all about him, life was good,
            But still he knew that he must fight,
              he must survive howe'er he could.

A sharpened stick to make a spear,
  a cave to hide himself therein,
    And there to shield from winter's blast,
      wrapped in another creature's skin.
        When heaven's lighting struck a fire,
          sly Man soon turned it to his use,
            To warm his cave, to cook his food;
              then with some creatures made a truce.

The dog, to help him with his kill,
  the horse to carry him with speed,
    With spear that struck down from afar,
      for might or fangs he had no need.
        The arrow soon replaced the spear,
          as man developed greater skill,
            Now Man no longer slew for food
              but for the pleasure of the kill.

The deer that roamed the forests deep,
  the seals that swam the icy fjord,
    The fish below, the birds above,
      Man was their master and their lord.
        And it was thus that Man began
          to violate all nature's plan;
            For with the power to smite at will,
              what greater prey was there than Man?

And in the years that followed,
  feud and warfare grew apace,
    As Man found ever swifter means
      to decimate the human race.
        Some lust for power, some fight for greed
          and some, they claim, for justice fair,
            While shells are fired and bombs are dropped,
              on land and sea and in the air.

So God's creation has become
　a demi-god in his own right,
　　With powers that rival nature's own,
　　which he will use to loot and fight.
　　　Someone has greater power or wealth
　　　and Man would grasp it if he can,
　　　　Yes, even tho' the cost might be
　　　　destruction of both Earth and Man.

The mountains too must yield their gold,
　and forests stripped of trees and seed,
　　The rivers choked, their waters fouled,
　　to satisfy Man's growing greed.
　　　For in his avarice Man has chosen
　　　to rape and plumb the bowels of Earth,
　　　　To fog the air, pollute the streams
　　　　and foul the soil that gave him birth.

For there are those who would believe
　there is no God, no master plan,
　　Who gaze at wonders all about
　　and claim all this as work of Man.
　　　Vain, foolish creature, oh so small,
　　　so miniscule in nature's pond,
　　　　Yet with the power now to destroy
　　　　the very Earth he stands upon.

And if in future times some race
　should reach this Earth and come to land,
　　They may well ask with some dismay,
　　　"What was this creature known as MAN?"

DISTURBING REFLECTIONS

As I strip for my shower each morning,
there's a guy in the mirror I see,
Now he has to be some elder cousin,
for I'm certain that guy can't be me.

I can see there's a family resemblance,
though he really looks more like my dad,
But he doesn't have my chiseled jawline
and his hair is receding quite bad.

Now common sense says that's my image
and they tell me that mirrors don't lie,
If so, what in Heaven's name happened
to that handsome and virile young guy?

For he sure doesn't bear much resemblance
to my wife's favorite picture of me,
Course I know it's some time since she took it,
the year was, I think, sixty-three.

So I gaze at the mirror in sorrow
and I ask what has happened since then,
To that fine, athletic young fellow
who could bench press two hundred and ten?

The legs are two muscular columns,
the delts and the pecs are just fine,
But what's that big roll 'round the middle?
Now surely, that cannot be mine!

Was it borrowed from some friendly camel
who had more than a little to spare?
Why on earth do they call them "love handles,"
and what happened to all of my hair?

I suppose I should not be complaining,
at least I'm not dead, I'm not ill,
But why is it when you pass forty,
the rest of the road is downhill?

At forty you've got it together,
at forty you're nobody's fool,
At forty, you know the whole game plan
and at that point they change all the rules.

At forty you realize you're slowing,
and you're losing a bit of your hair,
But you're so busy being successful
that at this point you simply don't care.

'Cause you know you still feel like a million
and your life is just peachy, so far,
Young girls are still turning and staring,
only now they're admiring your car.

At fifty, you smile at the ladies,
but it never works out as you've planned,
Though you once were a sexy young fellow,
you're now just a leering old man.

Unnoticed, the pounds come a-creeping,
though they're plain for all others to see,
Until one day you look in the mirror
and you shudder, "My god! Is that me?"

Then before you realize it you're sixty,
and you figure your life is near done,
Yet your heart is still strong and it's pumping,
and your legs aren't too feeble to run.

But now some young fellows are asking,
"Just who is that paunchy old clown?
I'd sure like the job that he's doing;
good lord, will he never step down?"

All too soon comes the time for retirement,
and your boss and the rest all feign grief,
But you hear, while you're cleaning your desk out,
someone give a big sigh of relief.

So this, you reflect, is retirement,
the golden time in a man's life,
No more need to toil for a living,
you can stay home and bother your wife.

Well my wife, at this point, is out shopping,
so I might as well have me a shower,
I'm alone and there's no one to bother
even if I should stay for an hour.

Because now that I have all this freedom,
I am no longer ruled by the clock,
And the mirror, by then, will be steamy,
and looking won't be such a shock.

A SENSE OF VALUES

I woke up this morning, lay there on my back
 and looked at the world through one eye,
As I gazed out the window I realized one fact,
 I really am a fortunate guy.

No, I don't have riches, nor castles in Spain,
 nor a yacht in the harbor, it's true,
But I sleep well at night and I don't have to fight
 for my wealth, the way some people do.

For my wealth is not the material sort,
 that a burglar might steal, should he try,
For the things that I value, some folks throw away,
 and they're all things that money can't buy.

Now the sunshine gives promise it will be a fine day,
 and there's a songbird out there in the tree,
I'm the only one here and to me it seems clear
 that the little guy's singing to me.

The house is all quiet and the sound that I hear
 is the coffee, just starting to perk,
And I give a quiet cheer for the weekend is here,
 and I've no need to go off to work.

I haven't a worry, a care or a pain,
 and I don't hate one soul on this earth,
And what I have gained seems, to me, very plain,
 when I think of the state of my birth.

I entered this world, not a stitch on my back,
 nor a pocket to put a dime in,
Not a cent to my name nor a hair on my head,
 all bare, with a big, toothless grin.

When you start off with nothing, it's darn hard to lose,
    no matter how hard you might try,
And you're bound to do great if your values are straight,
    for there's so much that money can't buy.

There's a fellow I know who is rolling in dough,
    and he dearly loves golf, there's no doubt,
But last weekend you see, after paying his fee,
    it poured and the game was rained out.

While in my backyard, where I loafed the whole day,
    there wasn't a cloud in the sky,
For the sun shines alike, on the rich and the poor,
    and that's one thing that money won't buy.

I've a friend down the road and he has a big load
    of problems and worries and such,
For while some guys I know have too little dough,
    this poor sucker has far too much.

Now he worries all day it will dwindle away,
    and he frets, as some rich people do,
That he'll reach his old age and he'll have to scrape by
    on only a million or two.

His worries and problems are ruining his health,
    he now has an ulcer, I hear,
And I can't help concluding that I'm better off,
    as I wash down my steak with some beer.

Now I don't have a mansion, like some of my friends,
    nor a mortgage at thirteen percent,
I don't owe the banks, and for this I give thanks,
    and I've no landlord screaming for rent.

I've a good wife who loves me, and not for my wealth,
    and my dog thinks that I'm quite a guy,
I'm as sound as a bell and my appetite's swell -
    Those are all things that money can't buy.

TOTAL CONTENTMENT

Now there have been times when I've written rhymes
That told of my carefree youth,
And I've written in prose, of friends and foes
And most, I will swear, was truth.
I have penned some lines about folks so fine
And a few who were quite uncouth.

I have made my call, with love for all,
Yes, even the woeful guy,
Whose soul is wracked with hatred black –
Do I hate him back? Not I!

For I know I will walk this route but once,
So I have no time for hate,
Or envy for that son-of-a-gun
Who has more dough and, perhaps, more fun,
'Cause the sun shines down on everyone,
And to me, life is simply great.

CHAPTER 6: *A TIME TO REMEMBER*

RETURN TO COVEY HILL

I journeyed today, back to old Covey Hill,
like a pilgrim in search of the truth,
Like the salmon that journeys back upstream to spawn,
I returned to the scene of my youth.

But there's darn little left of the place that I knew
and loved so when I was a child.
For the home I grew up in has been torn away
and the forest allowed to grow wild.

The bubbling brook where I fished as a lad
and the fields where I helped cut the hay,
Yes, all these are gone, like a moonbeam at dawn;
they are covered with spruces today.

There are two homes that stand, they are modern and grand,
each landscaped and with a fine lawn,
But that's all that remains of the place I once loved,
The rest of the old farm is gone.

Yes old Covey Hill has so drastically changed,
that I now find it hard to relate,
To the spot that I loved in the days of my youth,
as I linger awhile by the gate.

Just a short graveled road and a few stony farms,
hard living and most of us poor,
But our neighbors were friends who would stick to the end,
and very darn few locked their door.

I recall a small school, girls in gingham and bows,
boys in smelly old sneakers and jeans,
Where we learned the things that we needed to know
from a teacher not yet past her teens.

And the small church where folks went on Sunday to pray,
or some, for surcease from their toil,
There was darn little leisure in those distant days,
for those who survived on the soil.

But most of the farms are no longer in till,
gone for city folks' country estates,
And I paused awhile, sadly, on old Covey Hill,
'neath the maples that line the farm gate.

Well I guess that's progress; time cannot stand still
in a world full of turmoil and strife,
Still, I realize my youth spent on old Covey Hill
was the most carefree time of my life.

For I ran wild and free as a farm boy can be,
and of happiness I had my fill,
And I stole my first kiss, and I'll not name the Miss,
but it happened on old Covey Hill.

When I close my eyes I can see it again,
the farmhouse, the unpainted barn,
The big lazy farm dog, the old broody hen –
protecting her children from harm.

The Holsteins, the horses, the pigs in the pen,
and the rooster, so raucous, at dawn,
Yes these are the things I remember so well
from a youth that so quickly has gone.

The dark, brooding forest, the bubbling streams
I remember so well as a child,
A meadow surrounded by stone walls so high,
where strawberries used to grow wild.

The fireflies that sparkled the meadows at night,
and the cry of the lone Whip-poor-will,
And the birdsong, so sweet, at the breaking of day,
I remember from old Covey Hill.

But it seems all too soon I abandoned my youth,
turned my back on the quiet rural life,
For the lure of adventure and bright city lights,
and a lifetime of combat and strife.

There's a Will-of-the-wisp that entices us on,
staying ever just out of our grip,
Until we realize one day that a lifetime has passed
and that we've scarcely noticed the trip.

And the shine of the fool's gold that beckoned so bright
has dimmed with the passage of time,
And we now feel bereft for there's no challenge left,
and there're no further mountains to climb.

So I come back again to where it all began,
in search of a time I recall,
But the sounds of the silence are all that I hear
and the whisper of leaves as they fall.

Then a message, so softly invading my mind,
as I stand 'neath a great shady tree,
Seems I knew all along just what I would find,
there's no past here, there's nothing but me.

A wise man once said, "You can never go back,"
you and I know that that's the truth,
But you'll be disappointed; it's best not to try,
for you'll never recapture your youth.

So live for the present, the past is long dead
and the future an unwritten script,
And don't yearn for times you can never recall,
just enjoy every day of the trip.

REFLECTIONS

Forgotten is the endless work,
　　the unrelenting toil,
The poverty that seems to go
　　with working on the soil.

The blazing heat of Summer
and December's frigid clime,
The chronic lack of money;
that for ease, there's seldom time.

As you stand upon a hillside
　　in mid-September's sun,
And the changing colors warn you
　　that Summer's almost done.

And you glory in its beauty
　　and its panorama grand,
As you ponder at your folly,
　　why you ever left the land.

You recall a boy so happy –
　　barefoot, in ragged jeans.
Then the gnawing discontentment
　　of a young man in his teens,

Who could see the far horizons
and would know what lay beyond,
Who, in spirit of adventure,
packed his bag and then, was gone.

You recall the miles of travel
　　and the jobs that didn't last,
How you never made your fortune,
　　how the years flew by so fast.

And you wonder how you missed it,
why it took so long to see
That the man without a master,
is the man who's truly free.

There are some who say adventure
is the food that feeds the soul,
And the man who feels contentment
is a fool, or very old.

That the goal is not the winning,
but the challenge of the chase.
For we cannot all be winners,
but we all must join the race.

But you think of the frustrations
and the years of endless toil,
And the roots you never could put down
in any foreign soil.

You recall the fleeting friendships
and you realize the truth,
That the only ones that lasted,
were the friendships of your youth.

You remember frosty evenings
and the crispness of the morn,
And the rustle of the raccoons
as they foraged in the corn.

How you sensed the evening's coming
in the cooling western breeze,
And the pigeons flying homeward,
to their refuge in the trees.

You recall long days of labor
'neath the heat of Summer's sun,
And the weary relaxation
when the day was finally done.

Were you lured by hopes of riches,
to some far-off distant land?
Or the fear that in your father's home,
you ne'er become a man?

Perhaps it's human nature
that a man should ever long,
For the things he left behind him,
and to ask where he went wrong.

But for man to have a future,
he must ever have a goal,
And ignoring distant calling,
may well stultify the soul.

So you ask yourself this question,
"Am I happier today,
For leaving home and family
and for going my own way?"

And when you have your answer,
if it does not vex your soul,
You will know your life's successful
and you've truly reached your goal.

SPIDERS IN THE OUTHOUSE

It stood beyond the garden,
  underneath a shading pine,
    A tiny little outhouse
      which I always felt was mine.
        It has served its function, nobly
          I am sure, for many a year
            'Till my granddad built a bathroom
            and abandoned it, back here.

Where the pine tree helped support it
  and disguise its many leaks,
    And my granddad stored inside it
      bits of junk he called antiques.
        When I was a little shaver
          I complained, quite sad, one day,
            That my best friend had a treehouse,
            while I had no place to play.

So my granddad moved the junk out,
  patched some knot-holes in the floor,
    Put a little paint upon it
      and wrote "CLUBHOUSE" on the door.
        Very soon a club was meeting
          in my outhouse 'neath the tree,
            And of course I was the leader,
            since the place belonged to me.

Then the Spring moved into Summer,
  we discovered one warm day,
    That the outhouse had, as tenants,
      some fat spiders, big and gray.
        Who built their nests in corners
          to ensnare the buzzing flies,
            Or sometimes 'cross the doorway,
            just to catch us by surprise.

Now, I and my companions
  of our Clubhouse were quite proud,
    And as one, were in agreement,
      that no girls should be allowed.
        To profane these sacred quarters,
          where we boys most days did meet,
            To do the things that boys do,
              for this was our one retreat.

Still, there was no need to worry,
  once the news was noised around
    That the place was full of spiders,
      huge and hairy, gray and brown.
        Why no girl would venture near it,
          yes, of this we were quite sure;
            And I guess this was the reason
              why we never locked the door.

'Til the day that great-aunt Carey
  came to stay a week or two,
    And visit with her kin folk,
      as old aunts are wont to do.
        She went strolling through the garden
          in a reminiscent way,
            And she happened on the outhouse,
              while we children were away.

Well she knew its ancient purpose,
  and her eyesight was quite poor,
    So she failed to see the Clubhouse sign
      we'd written on the door.
        There was no one to observe her
          and the door was open wide,
            And she felt the call of nature,
              so great-auntie stepped inside.

She sat her down in comfort
and behind her latched the door,
To perform a private function,
as she'd done oft times before.
But just then two fat gray spiders
dropped down from overhead,
One landed upon auntie's thigh,
the other on her head.

It's hard to think that someone,
at the age of eighty-three,
Could scream so loud, or run as fast,
or jump as high as she.
I am told she cleared the garden hedge
with nigh an inch to spare,
And wound up in the kitchen,
with a spider in her hair.

It was thus I gained the knowledge
(which I never had been told)
That things that creep and things that crawl
are feared by young and old,
Of the feminine persuasion,
and this fact has served me well,
In spots and situations
far too numerous to tell.

There were incidents in childhood,
one or two of which I'll name,
When the odds were stacked in favor
of some pushy little dame,
When a beetle or an earthworm
the argument did sway,
And ended all discussion
in a full and final way.

Today, the modern woman
　is a wondrous thing to see,
　　She has a black belt in karate
　　　and, perhaps, a Ph.D.
　　　　And she's sure to win an argument
　　　　　opposed by any guy.
　　　　　　Still, I wonder if those lessons,
　　　　　　　learned in childhood, still apply?

Are they still afraid of spiders
　and of things that crawl or squirm?
　　Will they turn away and shudder
　　　at the wriggling of a worm?
　　　　And when the dew is heavy
　　　　　on the lushness of your lawn,
　　　　　　Will they help you pick up dew worms,
　　　　　　　in the hours preceding dawn?

In the battle of the sexes,
　with its constant pull and tug,
　　Does a man have a secret weapon
　　　in the common little bug?

THE PASSING

I entered into my son's room
and lay down upon his bed,
His books and trophies all around,
his dented pillow 'neath my head.

I cogitate while lying there,
how one small boy, now man full grown,
Has left his mark within this room
and ponder where the years have flown.

Recalling how his mom and I,
this room did fashion with such care,
And little knew, that day long past,
that he would grow to manhood there.

Nostalgically I gaze about
and finally, realize the truth,
That he has gone, but left behind
a poignant record of his youth.

The desk whereon he did his work,
a radio with batteries dead,
The nightstand small, that held his lamp
and underneath, the books he read.

A sloping closet 'neath the eaves,
a place to hide, a small boy's lair,
The door thereto I opened wide
and gazed at trophies lying there.

A small toy gun upon a belt,
a Crockett hat that he had worn,
A hockey stick with blade all scarred,
the comic books with pages torn.

Some skates, a cycle helmet too,
a favored jacket, tattered jeans,
All things of value and of worth,
owned by a young man in his teens.

All in a heap, abandoned there,
the story of one small boy's life,
From tiny lad to man full grown,
his triumphs, failures, toils and strife.

Then all too soon, he went his way
and left behind this empty spot,
To mark his passing through our lives;
this is, I know, a parent's lot.

To nurture, shelter and to teach,
to guide small feet and tiny hands,
Of little, helpless human things,
placed in our care by God's command.

Then, when their time has come to go,
release your hold with tact and grace,
And smile as they walk out the door
and leave behind a barren space.

THE OLD COPPER TUB

When I was a kid I lived on a farm,
we were poor and the living was hard,
For we hadn't a furnace or plumbing indoors,
just a privy out in the backyard.

Not having a bathroom, Mom needed a spot,
our poor little bodies to scrub,
So on Saturday night by the old kitchen stove
we were bathed in a big copper tub.

'Twas filled with warm water, we gathered around
then in turn all we kids would get in,
And with a stiff brush and some good yellow soap
Mom would scrub off the dirt and the skin.

First came little sister, then wee brother Will,
then finally, my turn came around,
And I'd jump in that tub to soak and to scrub,
in water quite muddy and brown.

Mom would stoke up the fire 'til the stove got quite hot
(of pneumonia she had a great fear)
As you stepped from the tub you were chilly in front
but toasted well done in the rear.

Once, I gave a great howl as I stooped for the towel,
after that life was never the same.
For my poor little bottom was branded for life
with the stove manufacturer's name.

Now each Monday morning 'twas filled to the brim
and Mom gave our clothing a scrub,
And on Wednesday Dad mixed up the feed for the stock,
(you guessed it) in the old copper tub.

The rest of the time it hung in the shed
and at noon, to call Dad for his grub,
Mom would take down a paddle that hung on the wall
and beat on the old copper tub.

I remember so well the Spring I was ten
and the stream by our house was in flood,
Little brother and I to go sailing did try
and we borrowed Mom's big copper tub.

So bravely we paddled out into the current,
not realizing that was a flub,
'Cause from three miles away we walked home that day
and we carried the old copper tub.

Since I have grown up life has treated me well,
I have prospered, yes that is the truth.
But one thing I have learned is that good times or bad,
you will always remember your youth.

So when nostalgia strikes I like to think back
to when I was a carefree young cub,
How I took my bath on a Saturday night
by the stove, in a big copper tub.

When my folks passed away and we sold the home farm,
the tub was battered and starting to leak;
So we gave it away to the fellow next door,
not realizing it was an antique.

Now I have a fine home and the bathtub I own
is the latest in modern design.
Still, I sometimes think back to that old copper tub
and reflect how it should have been mine.

So a few days ago I went into town,
to an antique house known as The Hub;
Where for three hundred dollars, a bargain I'm sure,
I bought back the old copper tub.

Boy! My wife sure got mad, she yelled I'd been had,
chased me out of the house with a club.
Still, I won't grieve, 'til she's over her peeve
I'll just sleep 'neath the old copper tub.

CHAPTER 7: *JUST FOR FUN*

THE OFFICE PARTY

When I woke up this morning, in my mouth there was a taste,
As though an aged ostrich had been sitting on my face.
As I staggered to the bathroom to find myself a pill,
(Getting up was painful, but then so was lying still).

I thought about the party and fun that I had had,
For after six martinis I am really quite a lad.
I hope my hostess doesn't know 'twas me who plugged the bowl,
When I changed the toilet paper and I dropped the entire roll.

And I hope nobody noticed my other little prank,
When I dropped a pickled herring with the goldfish in the tank.
The girl I spilled the cocktail on, I'd never seen before,
Think it was my Boss's sister; but really, I'm not sure.

And the fellow from accounting, I'm afraid I made him mad
When I said a guy as fat as he, should not be wearing plaid.
And now my wife is sore at me and she really can't be blamed,
Though it wasn't my suggestion that we start that parlor game.

I should not have grabbed the waitress (it was only done in play),
But she was serving canapés and dropped the entire tray.
And now I'm sick and sorry, and I'd like to make amends,
For embarrassing my hostess and insulting all my friends.

But then, if I apologize, I'm really in a mess,
'Cause for things they didn't notice, I'd be silly to confess.
But at the Boss's party (if they ask me back next year),
I'll stick to Perrier water, or perhaps a glass of beer.

BEANS

The logger in his mackinaw,
    the cowboy in his jeans.
        Have just one thing in common:
            they both love eating beans.

And that's why in the cook shack
    or out upon the range,
        You will always find some cooking,
            and nobody finds it strange.

As the cook prepares a pot of them,
    he sings a happy song,
        It won't be long 'til suppertime
            and the gang will be along.

There's cornbread in the oven
    and there's salt pork to be fried,
        And the coffee pot is boiling,
            while old Cookie beams with pride.

For he knows when supper's over,
    even though they've eaten most,
        He can serve what's left for breakfast,
            with some coffee and some toast.

Oh it's beans that keep the working man
    out there upon the job,
        In an air conditioned office
            they'd consider him a slob.

So the cowboy rides the prairies
and the logger falls the tree,
'Cause with all the beans they've eaten,
it's the only place to be.

The farmer out in rural Quebec,
wipes off his sweaty brow,
His wife, he knows, is baking beans,
they should be ready now.

With lots of maple syrup
and some pork rinds on the side,
It's food like this that makes him strong,
he'll tell you with some pride.

The Peon, down in Mexico,
in old straw hat and jeans,
Looks forward to his supper
of burritos made with beans.

While the lowly Russian laborer,
in the plant that makes the steel,
He knows black beans and cabbage soup
will be his evening meal.

For it's beans that fuel the working man
and strengthen up his spine,
But if he should bend over,
you should never stand behind.

Just keep him in the open air
    and give him lots of space,
        And he'll keep the country running
            with a smile upon his face.

Now we all know some health food nut
    who dines on fruit and greens,
        And dearly loves his tofu,
            which we know is made of beans.

While the poor old Newfie fisherman,
    who's not allowed to fish,
        I am told that beans and brevis
            has become his favorite dish.

Now the good folk down in Boston
    may be a bit uptight,
        But it's beans that made them famous,
            if my history book is right.

A plate of beans and bangers
    makes a London cockney smile,
        But steal a Cuban's refried beans
            and you're apt to drive him wild.

Oh, it's beans that feed the working man
    and keep the country strong,
        As long as we keep eating them,
            we know we won't go wrong.

And it's beans that keep the soldier, brave,
    advancing down the line,
        He'd rather face the enemy…
           'cause he knows what's behind.

So let's respect the noble bean
    and try to treat it fair,
        And just ignore the folks who say
           it harms the ozone layer.

It is, perhaps, the finest food
    that you will ever find,
        And is the one connecting link
           that binds all human kind.

For the Chinese eat them sprouted,
    while in Boston they are baked,
        In Quebec they're served with syrup
           and a piece of johnny cake.

And however far you travel,
    to whatever foreign scenes,
        If you stop to read a menu,
           I am certain you'll find beans.

JUST CHATTING

It's a beautiful day, the sun's shining,
    I decide that I'll go for a walk.
Then the phone rings, it's old Mrs. Lowry,
    she's lonely and just wants to talk.

So I foolishly ask her, "What's cooking?"
    and she tells me in minute detail.
For what others could say in one sentence
    to her is a serial tale.

It seems her best friend, Mrs. Jeffers,
    (I don't know the lady at all)
Decided to stroll through the market
    and had her a terrible fall.

She fractured her hip in three places,
    (and here, she describes the great pain)
But they've pinned it together with great metal pegs
    and they're certain she will walk again.

Mrs. Jeffers spent three hours in surgery,
    (she was not even properly dressed)
They never had seen such a fracture before
    and the doctors were all much impressed.

She pauses for breath and I ask her,
    "Mrs. Lowery, dear, how about you?"
You may not believe this next story,
    but I swear on my honor it's true.

For she tells me the saga of *Ripples*;
    Now Ripples, it seems, is her cat.
And she's very concerned, for poor Ripples
    has grown exceedingly fat.

But she feels that some background is needed
    so she talks, twenty minutes or more,
Of the kitten, half-starved and quite mangy,
    that somebody dropped at her door.

A she speaks of the poor thing's condition,
    I can sense that she's verging on tears.
Then she tells of the love and attention
    she has lavished on it o'er the years.

Now, the Vet says that Ripples must diet,
    and it really does seem such a shame;
Mrs. Lowery is feeling quite guilty
    for she feels she is really to blame.

An hour's passed (it really seems longer)
    and the dear old girl still prattles on,
And I hear of her poor neighbor's problem
    with the crabgrass that grows on his lawn.

And it seems a good friend has gone senile,
    he's thinking of buying a horse.
And her grand-niece, who lives in Miami,
    has finally filed for divorce.

Now I realize that two hours have flitted
    and, as yet, I've not got a word in.
But by now I have learned of her school chum
    who succumbed to that old devil, gin.

So I tell her the doorbell is ringing
    and I really must be on my way.
Now you ask, "How is dear Mrs. Lowery?"
    Well, truly, she never did say.

HONESTY DON'T PAY

We are told when we are children
   that lying is uncouth
      And we always should be truthful, if we can.
         But you're sure to get in trouble
           if you try to tell the truth,
              Because no one really trusts an honest man.

The guy that people seem to trust
   is not the honest man
      But a fellow who will look into your eyes,
         With a look of great sincerity
           and firmly clasp your hand
              While he tells to you the most outrageous lies.

Now it is my firm opinion
   that a man should never lie,
      That lying is bad-mannered and uncouth.
         But I can't stay out of trouble,
           however hard I try,
              Because no one ever wants to hear the truth.

My girl asked me if I loved her
   for her body or her mind,
      I was truthful as I'd always been before.
         When I said, her father's money,
           her reaction was unkind;
              She slapped my face and pushed me out the door.

An aunt asked my opinion
   of a hat that she had bought,
      And I swear I didn't mean to give offence,
         When I told her it reminded me
           of mother's chamber pot;
              But my auntie hasn't spoken to me since.

When looking for a job
  don't say you've just been fired,
    It really is much safer if you lie.
      If you say you ran the company,
        you'll probably get hired
          And your boss will brag that you're a macho guy.

When they ask you for a resume
  of things that you have done,
    Be sure to tell a whopper, if you can.
      For the plain unvarnished truth, my friend,
        is never any fun
          And no one will believe a truthful man.

If you run for public office
  there's a very simply ploy
    That politicians use with great success.
      It's to simply tell the people
        the thing they most enjoy,
          That they're different, more deserving than the rest.

We know that politicians
  get along so well in life
    'Cause they tell the people what they want to hear.
      Though they never keep their promises,
        they still stay out of strife
          And we suckers re-elect them, year by year.

So this little bit of wisdom
  I would like to pass along
    And I grieve I didn't learn it in my youth;
      If you want the world to love you
        and to really get along
          For goodness sake, don't ever tell the truth.

THE STABBING OF THE HAGGIS

A friend one day invited me
to drop down to the hall,
Where in honor of the Scottish bard,
they planned to have a ball.
For it would stir my torpid soul,
he told me with a grin,
When, to the skirling of the pipes,
they brought the haggis in.

I confess I knew but little
of the poet, Robbie Burns
Or even what a haggis was,
but felt 'twas time I learned.
So although I have no Scottish blood,
I felt t'would be alright,
And in my best blue serge
I went to the hall that night.

Now the thing that most surprised me
as I walked into the hall,
Was the fact that many men there
had no trousers on at all.
My friend, he then assured me
it was indeed the plan,
That those with Scottish forbears
wear the tartan of their clan.

Now I couldn't claim a tartan
and for this I was quite pleased,
For I knew at least my trousers
hid the hair upon my knees.
So I sat down at a table
with my back toward a wall,
And 'twas then I saw the piper
just beyond me in the hall.

With the pipes slung o'er his shoulder
and his drone pipes all a'tilt,
He'd an honor guard behind him
and they all were wearing kilts.
The piper spanked the bagpipes,
they began to squeal and wail,
Much as a little pig might
if you trod upon his tail.

The chanter and the drone pipes
then joined in mournful dirge,
And to leave the pipers presence,
I confess, I felt an urge.
Into the hall the entourage
then marched with pomp and state,
The piper and the escorts
and the haggis, on a plate.

The piper and the honor guard
wore kilts and fancy dress,
While on the plate the haggis lay,
a sodden, lumpy mess.
They marched to the head table where,
with some grace and flair,
'Twas presented to a fellow
who I saw was standing there.

Who then addressed the haggis
and I'll not repeat the words,
For he spoke a foreign language
that I'd hitherto not heard.
The words he used were not in French,
now that much I could tell,
And I'm certain they weren't in English
for that language I know well.

He spoke to it with reverence
as one might address a king,
While on the plate the haggis lay,
and answered not a thing.
He then removed a dagger
from the waistband of his kilt,
And in the poor wee haggis,
he plunged it to the hilt.

Then, as the crowd applauded,
why he looked about and said,
"You realize I did that
to make sure the damn thing's dead."
A diner turned to me and asked,
"Is there any Scotch in you?"
I replied, "I've had a double,
but I think I'll make it two."

As I sat and sipped my whiskey,
humming Scotland the Brave,
I could sense my Gallic forbears
turning slowly in their graves.
And as the scotch soaked in
and I began to get a glow,
I felt sorry for the haggis
who'd been dealt a mortal blow.

So I'll make a small confession,
even though it causes pain,
Though the party was quite pleasant,
I would not go back again.
For it is my firm opinion
that it takes no courage, great,
To stab a little haggis,
lying helpless, on a plate.

CHAPTER 8: FAMILIES, NEAR AND FAR

THE LEAVING

The children have grown up and scattered
to far distant points of the earth,
All that's left is the father who sired them
and the mother who gave them their birth.

And the souvenirs of their childhood,
all these things that we can't throw away,
They've been left in our care, we must guard them,
who knows? they may want them some day.

There's the bikes and the skis and the records,
and a drum set that's gathering dust,
And we leave them and just work around them,
after all, they were left here in trust.

We can't very well just discard them,
that would not seem the right thing to do.
They're the only link left to our family,
and the full, busy life we once knew.

There are toys tucked away in the attic,
we look at them now and again;
They remind us that once there were children,
who, too soon, grew up to be men.

Our rec' room that once was so cluttered,
is now just as neat as can be,
And the home that was once full of people,
contains now, just my wife and me.

The house is so silent it echoes,
how well I recall how it rung,
With their laughter, their horseplay, their music,
when we and our children were young.

Oh, I know that kids all have to grow up,
and find their own place in the sun;
Still, it's hard not to feel kind of let down,
when you realize your life's work is done.

Well maybe some day, if we're lucky,
some grandkids may just come along.
Then this old house will, once more, be ringing
with the horseplay and laughter and song.

ADVICE TO A SON

You say you need no one, that you are a man
 and can make it quite well on your own,
But you have a long route ahead of you, son –
 much too far to travel alone.

From the home of your parents to one of your own,
 and the knowledge that you are a man,
To the freedom you have from the love you have known,
 is sometimes a terrible span.

No man is an island, so goes the old saw,
 and those you have lived know it's true,
And life's heavy burdens which now weigh you down,
 are lighter, divided by two.

If it's only a hand you can clasp in the dark,
 or a warm, loving voice on the phone,
Which says you're important and that you have worth –
 it surely beats being alone.

Don't punish yourself for mistakes in your past,
 don't say you can never go home,
But look for that someone who'll share your long path,
 for it's too lonesome walking alone.

The star that you follow, you may never reach,
 but you'll know, at life's end, that you tried;
And that, on your way, you'd the love and support
 of the person who walked by your side.

So don't try to do it, son, all on your own,
 for that path should be trodden by two;
And somewhere out there is a person who'll share –
 that someone who's just right for you.

THE OLD MAN

His shoulders are stooped and his hair's getting thin
and he don't move as fast as he did,
But he was the guy who stood seven feet tall
when you were a wee little kid.

In a world full of terrors, you always felt safe
long as you had hold of his hand,
For then he was Poppa or Daddy or Dad,
but now he is just the old man.

Remember the guy who excused your misdeeds
by saying that, "Boys will be boys?"
Who painted your bike and patched your skinned knees
and repaired all your broken down toys?

Remember the guy on whose shoulders you sat
so that you could look over the crowd?
And don't be ashamed if he tells a tale twice;
Just say, "he's my Dad," and be proud.

There's the time you went camping and he taught you to fish,
that summer when you were a lad.
And you slept 'neath the stars that night, by a stream;
just you and your best friend, your dad.

And when your first romance went badly askew
and didn't work out as you'd planned,
And you needed advice and a comforting word
and you went to, that's right! the old man!

When the hugs that he gave you, when you were a child,
were replaced by the clasp of his hand;
You knew that he loved you not one bit the less.
He was still there, he was your old man.

And though there were times when you might disagree,
you knew he would still back your stand.
For when push came to shove, he was always right there
in your corner, there stood the old man.

But now you've outshone all the things that he's done,
you've surpassed him in knowledge and wealth.
Now you are the one who stands straight and tall,
while he's stooped and failing in health.

So take him to lunch or buy him a beer,
and call him whenever you can.
Who knows if he'll even be with you next year;
and remember, he is The Old Man.

THE LONGEST STEP

I'm far from home and I'm all alone
    and God, but the days are long,
        And I think of my family and childhood friends
        and wonder if I did wrong.

The city lights all glitter so bright
    when you see them from far away,
        But I never dreamed it would be like this
        and I'm not sure I want to stay.

No trees, no flowers, only concrete towers
    as far as the eye can see,
        There's a city out there but it doesn't care
        'bout a small town boy like me.

For the teeming mobs have no time to talk
    or to pass the time of day,
        And suddenly home seems awfully dear
        and so very far away.

I wonder what Dad is doing now?
    He's probably watching the news,
        Bet the dog is lying beside his chair
        and he's maybe kicked off his shoes.

I promised Dad that I'd paint the porch
    before I left last fall,
        But the weather got bad, I ran out of time
        and it never got done at all.

I never did tell my Mom and Dad
   how much I appreciate
      All those things they did for so many years,
         Ah well, it's still not too late.

Bet they'd be surprised if I turned up
   with my suitcase in my hand,
      I know I'd be welcome, still I can't go;
         gotta prove that I'm a man.

Guess I should write them a letter tonight
   and let them know I'm okay,
      The trouble is I'm feeling so down
         I'm not certain what I'd say.

I really should wait a couple of days
   and then write a letter home,
      Maybe by then I'll have a job
         and I won't feel so alone.

Then I'll tell them about the city, grand
   and I'll say that I'm having fun,
      And even though I'm a full grown man
         I'll sign it, "Your loving son."

THE BOND

Our little boy was all tucked in,
I sat beside him on his bed,
He looked at me with trusting grin,
"Tell me a story, Dad," he said.

And so I spun the lad a tale
of heroes, scaling mountains steep;
He did not ask if it was true,
just snuggled down and went to sleep.

But in his dreams that night, I'm sure,
were mountains tall, with snow-capped peaks,
That he did climb with trusted friends,
for small boys must adventure seek.

My small son joined me on the roof
and stood, with hammer in his hand,
"I've come to help you, Dad," he said,
"For very soon I'll be a man."

"And when I am a man full grown,
then I must know the things men do.
So I won't play with friends today,
instead I'll stay and work with you."

We toiled all day, 'neath summer's sun,
drove nails and chatted, man to man,
And when at last the job was done,
he smiled and said, "Today's been grand."

And when that night, I tucked him in,
"Did I do good today?" he said,
I answered, "Yes," he smiled with pride
and snuggled, weary, in his bed.

And did his dreams that night, perchance
include a mansion, tall and grand,
That he would build some future day
when he was finally a man?

"My bike tire's flat," he said one day,
"But if you'll show me what to do
I can repair it by myself
and I won't have to bother you."

And as we worked upon his bike,
discussing many projects grand,
A man reliving boyhood dreams,
a boy who longed to be a man.

I told him then of my own youth,
it seemed so very long ago,
There was no on to teach me then,
the things that every boy should know.

'Twas in these times a bond was formed,
not shared by mother or by wife,
A bond so rare 'twixt man and son
that comes so rarely in one's life.

A man full grown, he sought me out,
"I need advice once more," he said.
"I've met a girl and we're in love,
do you think I'm too young to wed?"

The pride I felt upon that day
may well sustain me all my life.
That this young man, so sure and strong,
should seek my counsel on a wife.

His knowledge now exceeds my own,
his wealth as well, of this I'm sure.
And to a far place he has gone,
he comes to seek advice no more.

But still my chest swells with the pride
a man may feel at work well done,
For to the world he is a man,
but still to me, he is my son.

GOD BLESS THE CHILDREN
(A GRANDFATHER'S PRAYER)

God bless our grandson, all safe in his bed,
With two loving parents to see he's all right.
Please God, help the children who have no one to love them,
The ones who are homeless or hungry, tonight.

Bless all the children, those unwanted ones,
Who are desperately seeking for someone to care.
Protect those small angels who are being abused,
By adults, uncaring, who have no love to share.

All that we ask is you guard well the children,
In a world full of hazards, make certain they thrive.
And shelter them well, these innocent angels,
For these are our future, are we to survive.

In the depths of the jungle that we call a city,
Where evil runs rampant, Lord shelter them well,
From the grasp of all beasts with evil intentions,
Who call themselves men but are creatures from Hell.

Give parents the wisdom to think of their children,
Not use them as pawns if a marriage goes wrong.
But learn to respect their love for both parents,
And give them a chance to grow up straight and strong.

Lord shelter the children in all far-off countries,
From the madness of war and the evil of hate.
Give adults the wisdom to stop all the slaughter,
And think of their children before it's too late.

And finally, Lord, please look in on our grandson,
Oh I know he's loved and I know he's all right.
But he's so far away and, well, I sort of miss him,
So give him a kiss from his Grandpa, tonight.

CHAPTER 9: THE PEACEFUL LIFE

CHILDHOOD RECOLLECTIONS

There's a little old log cabin on a hill, beside a wood
And a brook that runs beside it, I recall,
And I still can hear the rushing of that brook, in early Spring
And see the changing colors in the Fall.

I remember well my bedroom in the attic, 'neath the eaves,
It was smaller than most bathrooms are today.
But I had a wood to roam in and a stream where I could swim,
And a hundred acre farm on which to play.

I had a big, black collie and he was my closest friend,
He would sneak upstairs whene'er he had the chance,
And when the house had quieted down, he'd slip into my room
And sleep beside my bed, upon my pants.

We would roam the fields in Autumn,
Catching field mice, chasing squirrels,
Flushing partridge from the spruces on the hill,
While the frosty air of Autumn turned the leaves to red and gold
And was followed all too soon by Winter's chill.

In my bed beneath the rafters, with the covers o'er my head
I would lie and listen to the Winter's storm.
And I still recall the snowdrifts that piled up around the door,
And the wood we burned to keep the cabin warm.

There was hard work then in plenty, and never too much dough
And getting through the Winter was a fight.
I recall my mother saying, "If we make it until Spring,
When the grass turns green why, then we'll be alright."

Oh! I know by modern standards we were poor as one can be,
　　　The trouble was we didn't know it then.
Because all around were neighbors who were just as poor as we,
　　　And we had to help each other now and then.

You might trade a load of cordwood for half a side of beef,
　　　Or some chickens for a ton or two of hay.
For although it was Depression and we didn't have relief,
　　　Somehow it seemed we always found a way.

In our little church at Christmas, with its tinseled Christmas tree
　　　Was a pasteboard box, set just inside the door,
With a sign that asked for money for those less well off than we,
　　　And we always had a bit, to help the poor.

We were poor but we were happy,
　　　with our families and our friends
As we wrested out a living from the soil,
With no unions there to tell us how exploited we had been,
　　　How the Bosses took the profit of our toil.

And I cannot help but wonder, as I view today's unrest,
　　　With the strikes and unions screaming, ever, 'More,'
While we go in debt to pay for things that we don't really need
　　　And I wonder, is it better to be poor?

Today the rich aren't happy and the poor are ill content,
　　　While the middle class, who carry all the load,
Complain of rising taxes and the government's intent
　　　To put the whole darn Nation on the road.

Seen through the eyes of childhood, life takes on a rosy glow,
　　　Memory's vision sometimes differs from the truth.
But while life has imperfections, there is one thing that I know,
　　　There is happiness in innocence and youth.

BOYHOOD DREAMS

We sat by the bank of a rippling brook,
    Rusty, Charlie and me,
And we rested our backs on an old stone well
    'neath a spreading maple tree.

And we watched the minnows dart around,
    tossed stones in a sun-kissed pool,
As we made our plans for the years ahead
    when finally we'd left school.

Discussing the things we would like to do
    as we whiled the time away,
And our plans were grand and our plans were broad
    on that beautiful autumn day.

Not for us such mundane things
    as a job, a home and a wife;
But high adventure in foreign lands
    as we lived the fast-lane life.

And like the birds that circled above,
    we vowed we'd be strong and free,
And never be bound by things or time,
    not Rusty, Charlie or me.

But Rusty died in an auto crash
    before he was even a man.
Chuck joined the Army and gave his life
    in a far-off, distant land;

And I never did get to write the book
    that would bring me wealth and fame,
For when Boys grow up the world must change
    and is nevermore the same.

And you live your life and you do what you must,
    as the Gods of fate decree,
Tho' you've made your plans by a flowing brook,
    like Rusty, Charlie and me.

I'll not complain for my life's been good,
    tho' the years have flown so fast,
And the gray in my hair reminds me now
    that much of my life is past.

And what I've acquired is a loving wife
    and some children who do me proud,
A routine job and an average life,
    and I'll never stand out in the crowd.

But sometimes in moments of solitude
    I remember that sun-kissed pool,
Where we used to stop and visit awhile
    on our way back home from school.

I can feel the heat of the autumn sun,
    hear the sounds of the birds on high,
And still remember the plans we made,
    Rusty, Charlie and I.

I'd like to go back to that stream once more
    on a beautiful Autumn day;
Just lean my back to that old stone wall
    and while an hour away.

To see if the minnows still dart about
    and the birds still circle, free,
And dream once more of three good friends,
    Rusty, Charlie and me.

REMINISCENCE

We're just lying here, old Ranger and me,
Side by side 'neath a big shade tree,
Dreaming of how things used to be,
But now we're getting old.

Two hundred acres of rolling land,
Now there was really a job for a Man,
The kind of work that the Maker planned,
But now, we're just too old.

For thirteen years he walked by my side,
Sometimes trotting to meet my stride,
Doing a farm dog's job with pride,
And now we're both getting old.

I wonder now, who's tilling the soil,
Where me and my family used to toil;
Or maybe they're just drilling holes for oil,
'Cause that's the way of the world.

And now he's gazing off into space,
With a wistful look upon his face,
Maybe he's thinking about the race
He had with a woodchuck one day.

Now my kids are gone and my grandkids too,
And there isn't too much for me to do,
Except to sit here and talk with you,
My faithful, hairy old friend.

Remember how we hunted 'coon
By the light of a big September moon?
It's a shame that it all had to end so soon,
But we've both gotten old, my friend.

Yes I'm getting tired and I'm feeling low,
And you're getting kind of lame and slow,
And I'm wondering, who'll be the first to go?
Will it be you or me, my friend?

I'm thinking now of your seventh year,
When you were gored by the neighbor's steer.
How you stood your ground and didn't show fear,
Yes, you were one hell of a dog.

From dangerous jobs, you never shrunk,
Why, one day you even took on a skunk.
Boy! I still remember the way you stunk.
Remember that, old friend?

Yes, we've both had our turn in the Sun,
And some was hard work, but a lot was fun,
And it's hard to believe that it's all done,
'Cause we've both been retired, my friend.

Now I'm going to leave you here alone,
While I get me a beer, and you a bone,
But first, go and chase that cat back home,
'Cause that's still your job, my friend.

FARMER'S SON

Dad knocked on my door one dark, rainy morn,
    I remember 'twas only just dawn;
He said, "Roll out son, we must go on a hunt
    And find out where Bessie has gone."

Bessie, you see, was an old jersey cow,
    She was stubborn, cantankerous and wise,
And she liked to sneak off, have her calf in the woods,
    All alone, far from our prying eyes.

Well! I looked out the window at the rain pouring down
    And I pictured that rain on my head,
And I thought of my cousin who lived in the Town
    All snuggled down safe in his bed.

I pulled on my jeans, my slicker and hat,
    My gumboots and all of the rest,
And I stepped out the door and I asked, "Lord, why me?"
    As I set out to search for old Bess.

Now our pasture was wooded, our pasture was rough,
    It was not your typical lawn;
As I stumbled along, over stones and through brush,
    I wondered where Bessie had gone.

Was she on the east side? Was she on the west?
    Was she away back in the bog?
And the rain, from my slicker, ran right down my boots,
    Then I tripped and fell over a log.

As I got to my feet (I was soaked to the skin)
    And I searched through that forest of green,
And I stumbled and swore as I looked for that cow,
    But Bessie was not to be seen.

Then 'neath a big hemlock that held back the rain,
    Stood Bessie, all wet and forlorn,
And there at her feet lay a little bull calf,
    Half drowned and not many hours born.

Well I scooped the little guy up in my arms
    And I started on back to the barn,
And Bessie, she trod right close on my heels
    Making sure that he came to no harm.

But to carry a calf down the side of a hill,
    In the rain, I will swear is no fun,
For he seemed to gain ounces with each step I took,
    'Til it felt like he weighed half a ton.

When I came to the creek that ran 'cross our farm
    I decided I wouldn't go 'round,
For that bull calf gained weight with each step that I took
    And the bridge was a quarter mile down.

So I waded in, but the stream was in flood
    And I hadn't crossed much more than half,
When I slipped and fell flat on my face, in the mud,
    Right on top of that poor little calf.

I got to my feet, bent to pick the calf up,
 But before I had even a chance,
Why Bessie, she lowered her bony old head
 And she butted me right in the pants.

On my feet once more, I headed for shore
 But I'd lost my left boot in the flood.
When I got to dry land, I had only one boot
 And a sock that was covered with mud.

Well, the calf reached the shore and old Bessie crossed o'er
 And there, on the bank, made her stand,
Determined, it seemed, to protect her wee babe
 From this reckless and clumsy young man.

Now Bess wouldn't move to I twisted her tail
 Determined I'd get her to go,
But she simply stepped back with her big, cloven hoof
 And placed it atop my big toe.

Well enough is enough! So I grabbed up a stick
 And I beat on her bony, old stern,
With a leap and a lurch she took off for the barn
 And I hoped that her lesson she's learned.

The bull calf and I, we followed along,
 Wet, muddy, a little forlorn,
On four cloven hooves and one rubber boot
 And a sock that was tattered and torn.

I got to the stable and put them inside,
    Then I closed the barn door with a thud,
Deciding, right there, that I'd had quite enough
    Of cows and frustration and mud.

Today as I sit here, I think of the farm
    And the feel of the grass 'neath my feet.
But I traded it all for a seat at a desk
    And a window that looks on the street.

Sometimes I long for my old working clothes
    And the smell of the freshly cut hay,
'Stead of carbon monoxide that stings in my nose
    And the roaring of traffic each day.

Well, we all have to grow up and follow our star
    Still, I'd like to go back, if I could,
To when I was a boy, so carefree and young,
    Out hunting a calf in the wood.

SONG OF A LAZY FARMER

I'm sitting beneath a big shade tree,
   As contented as beast or man can be,
      Oh! I know that it's only a quarter-to-three,
        And I should be at work, that's plain.

My wife says that I should get me hence,
   And mow the weeds by the pasture fence,
      But to me that don't make a lick of sense,
        'Cause they'll just grow back again.

Now I'm aware that my neighbors say,
   I'm too lazy to give 'em the time of day,
      And I'd rather go fishing than cut my hay.
        Well! that's just the way I'm made.

I know in the Bible, somewhere it's said,
   That a man's got to sweat for his daily bread,
      But when that sun starts beating down on my head,
        I know where there's lots of shade.

Yeah! I know that the place is getting run down
   And the barn is tumbling into the ground,
      But by the time it falls, I won't be around,
        So why should it worry me?

They say what you sow is what you reap,
   Now that may be okay when labor's cheap,
      But today it's a way to lose a heap
        By hiring help, you see.

I figure I got no reason to whine,
    I got twelve cows and they're milking fine,
        And my farm is small but at least it's mine.
            Yes, I'm a contented man.

While my old friend, Bob, who lives next door
    Has four hundred acres and still wants more,
        'Though I think he's nuts, at seventy-four
            To be buying up more land.

No, I don't envy old Bob next door
    Even though he's rich and I'm kind of poor,
        'Cause he works 'til dark, then he does his chores
            And by then I'm watching T.V.

And that hump on his back sure does look queer,
    It's caused by too much hard work, I fear.
        I've a bump in the front, but that's caused by beer,
            And it doesn't worry me.

Now he bought him a combine and that's all right,
    But the interest rose to a helluva height
        And the end of his debt's nowhere in sight;
            He's a mighty worried man.

'Cause he's seventy-four and he's working yet
    To service the interest on that debt,
        And when he kicks off, I'm willing to bet
            He'll still owe a hundred grand.

They say farm improvement's the way to go,
    The government helps you to borrow the dough,
        But the banks foreclose if your payments are slow.
        Now that's not the life for me.

But I built me a pond 'cause I've no doubt
    It'll come in handy in times of drought,
        And the government stocked the thing with trout,
        'Cause I like to fish, you see.

So I work a little and fish my pond
    And enjoy my life 'cause when I'm gone,
        I know somehow they'll carry on
        Without my helping hand.

And the next guy who owns this farm
    Can paint the house and repair the barn,
        Or let it fall in, I don't give a darn.
        I just hope he's a happy man.

CHAPTER 10: *A TIME FOR CELEBRATION*

RÉVEILLON – A French-Canadian all-night party, held on Christmas Eve after midnight Mass, when family and relatives congregate at one home (usually the grandparents') for a night of fun and revelry.

A CHRISTMAS RÉVEILLON

'Twas the night before Christmas back home on the farm,
And the wood stove was roaring to keep the house warm.
Papa in his nightshirt and Maman in her hat,
Had just wound up the clock and had put out the cat.

I had turned down the covers and was just sliding under,
When someone knocked on the door and it sounded like thunder.
Papa looked out the window and I heard him swear,
"Well, sacre maudit, it's your big brother, Pierre."

"Should we let him in?" he asked of Maman,
"He's carrying gifts and some good whiskey blanc."
She opened the door up, but then Maman said,
"It's very late, Pierre, we're just going to bed."

Well, Uncle Pierre laughed and he said, "Yes, I know,
But it's your turn this year to hold *Réveillon*.
We would have held it, but our house is small,
While your house is big and there's room for us all.
Aunt Denise has the turkey, Maman the tortière
And you'd better get dressed 'cause they're all coming here."

Well the first to arrive was our fat cousin, Rose,
And she kissed all the family before wiping her nose.
She had the twins with her, which was not at all strange,
I could tell by the smell they both needed a change.

Then cousin Jean-Paul, who is just five foot two,
He brought the beer and it was all he could do
To carry two cases from the truck to the door,
He said, "If that's not enough I can go back for more."

Aunt Denise then came in with a turkey so big,
That Papa remarked 'twas the size of a pig.
She laughed, "We'll have time for some drinking and fun,
Then we'll all eat well when the turkey is done."
Theophile had his fiddle, Aunt Claire had some spoons,
And we knew we were in or some old-fashioned tunes.

Then came Uncle Paul and his daughter, Celine,
And I stopped feeling grouchy and started to grin.
She kissed all the family and that was real nice,
And I felt pretty good, because me she kissed twice.
Theophile took his fiddle and started a tune,
While Aunt Claire joined in with a couple of spoons.

Then Uncle Pierre said, "That makes me want to dance,"
So he jumped to his feet and he started to prance.
Uncle Pierre's a big man and he has a large belly,
That shook when he danced like a bowl full of jelly.
Then Maman cried out, "You know Pierre, you're not small,
And you're shaking the pictures all down off the wall!"

Old Joe, he got drunk (he's the family disgrace),
Sneaked into the kitchen with a grin on his face.
And Grandmère remarked, "A good thing I went in,
He was basting the turkey with a bottle of gin."

Grandpère was playing with the kids, in the hall,
They were shouting and laughing and having a ball.
They were getting real noisy when I heard Maman yell,
"What are you kids up to, what's that awful smell?"
I was going to tell her but before I could start
One kid laughed, "It's Grandpère, he just made a big fart."

It was a fine party, of that there's no doubt,
Because nobody left, although several passed out.
And we sang the old songs that we all knew so well,
We drank and we danced and raised all sorts of Hell.

We ate up the turkey and drank all the beer,
Wished each other *"Bonne Fete,"*
and said, "See you next year."
And Celine remarked as she gave me a kiss,
"What a shame *Les Anglais* don't have parties like this."

COMING HOME FOR CHRISTMAS

They're coming home for Christmas,
    some from many miles away.
        They've already phoned to tell us
            they'll be home for Christmas Day.

Bearing gifts, some bringing girlfriends,
    (Lord!) where will we put them all?
        Guess we'll have to set up camp cots,
            in the basement or the hall.

Yes, their friends will all be calling;
    there'll be such a carry on,
        Catching up on news and gossip –
            all that's happened since they've gone.

We'll dust off the old piano,
    fill the fridge with things to eat,
        Then await the gang's homecoming –
            Ah! That will be such a treat.

This old house has been so silent
    since the boys all went away,
        And we're really looking forward
            to their coming, Christmas Day.

Songs and fun, the sound of laughter,
    lots of good old-fashioned noise...
        To the world they're men all grown up,
            but to us they're still the boys.

Yes, they're coming home for Christmas,
   get the baking under way;
      Buy the turkey, wrap the presents,
         get prepared for Christmas Day.

Let us find once more the pleasure
   that we knew when they were young,
      And the joy we felt at Christmas,
         when the house, with laughter, rung.

For will there be many more times,
   now they've gone so far away,
      When they'll set aside their business
         and come home on Christmas Day?

SNOW FOR CHRISTMAS

Well, it's finally snowing for Christmas,
Light and fluffy as icing on cakes;
As it covers the yard and the hedges,
Lord! What a picture it makes.

It weighs down the pine and the spruces,
Lays a blanket o'er meadow and field,
And it looks like a painting by Rockwell,
Too clean and too white to be real.

On our front lawn, the shrubs and the rosebush
Are outlined in silhouette, bold,
Did God give us all of this beauty
In exchange for discomfort and cold?

The trees on the lawn, Christmas lighted,
And embellished with caplets of white,
Give the whole town a fairyland aspect,
As we walk down the streets, late at night.

Our friends to the south well may scorn us,
For living in a climate like this,
But those who flee southward for winter,
Little know of the beauty they've missed.

Today's plans, "Fly now and pay later,"
Put the sun within everyone's reach,
But I wouldn't trade my White Christmas
For the heat and the sand of a beach.

A FINAL THOUGHT

NOSTALGIA

As the months add up and the years roll by
I realize more and more,
That my days on this earth are passing by
and my time could soon be o'er.

I can't complain, for my life's been good,
and regrets, I have but few.
But before I depart from this earthly place
there are things I have yet to do.

Tho' I lay no claim to wealth or fame
still, life has not passed me by,
For I was born a country boy
and a country boy I'll die.

Big city life with its toil and strife,
I chose for myself, and yet,
As my mind slips back to my carefree youth,
there are things that I can't forget.

So I must go back to the old home farm
again, just one more time,
To dabble my feet in a babbling brook
and find a tree to climb.

Yes, I must go back to the farm again,
before I am too old,
To wade, barefoot, in a bullrush'd swamp
and catch me a frog to hold.

I must return to where I carved my name
on a bole of a big beech tree,
And lie at rest in a leaf-filled nest
that is known to only me.

To lie on my back in a field once more
on a beautiful summer's day,
While I turn my face to the cloudless sky
and smell the fresh-cut hay.

There is life that teems in the woods and streams,
while birdsong fills the air;
And I'll hear the knell of a far church bell
as I lie so peaceful there.

Perhaps if I simply close my eyes,
let imagination stray,
Some kindly elf may transport me back
to a far gone, distant day;

When I was a boy, without a care,
whose journey had just begun.
And I'll savor once more those days of yore,
when all was freedom and fun.

But if I should gaze in the limpid pool
beneath that old beech tree,
There'll be an old guy staring back,
and I'll know that guy is me.

Or perhaps if I lie on a leafy bed
and gaze at a cloudless sky,
I'll see, once more, those comrades of yore –
perhaps they'll come strolling by.

And the present day will fade away
like a dream that's not meant to be,
As my childhood friends all gather 'round
and they'll be as young as me.
And we'll sit and we'll talk of our future plans
for a life that is yet to be.

So I must go back to the farm again,
before I am to old –
To relive, once more, a carefree time,
and perhaps, restore my soul.

ABOUT THE AUTHOR

LARRY VAINCOURT

Award-winning columnist Larry Vaincourt has previously published two successful volumes of prose and poetry: **RHYMES AND REFLECTIONS** and **DON'T BURN THE BIFFY**. He is best known for his moving poem **JUST A COMMON SOLDIER (A Soldier Died Today)**, which has been reprinted thousands of times worldwide.

Born in upstate New York, Larry grew up as a farm boy in the rural setting of Covey Hill, Quebec, where he lived until he joined the Air Force in World War II as a Leading Aircraftsman. After serving as an aircraft mechanic and part-time entertainer, he returned to Quebec in 1946.

He has had a varied career that has included working as a logger, news photographer (ABC News Pictures), civil servant and metallurgical photographer (Rolls Royce).

In 1963 Larry opened his own photo studio, which he operated until 1983. After selling the business Larry embarked upon his writing career, first as a regular columnist for **THE LACHUTE WATCHMAN**.

His prose and poetry currently appear in the Canadian journals **DIALOGUE** and **MAIN STREET,** and can also be read on his web site. For many years his poetry also appeared on the **CBC** (Canadian Broadcasting Corporation) program **FRESH AIR**.

Larry and his wife Doreen celebrated their 50th wedding anniversary on September 1st, 2001.

Larry received the **2004 Column of the Year Award** from the Quebec Community Newspapers Association.

Made in the USA
Columbia, SC
06 February 2022

55586591R00085